Mountaineering in Patagonia

Mountaineering in Patagonia

by

Alan Kearney

CLOUDCAP

Mountaineering in Patagonia

Published by CLOUDCAP, Box 27344, Seattle, Washington 98125

Manufactured in the United States of America

ISBN 0-938567-30-6

Table of Contents

PATAGONIA

KILOMETERS

0 100 200 300

From original map by Gino Buscaini

INTRODUCTION

by
Chris Jones

Patagonia exerts a powerful impact on us. It has not only great physical beauty, but also a tangible presence. This presence is due in part to the remoteness and loneliness of the land, and in part to the storms and clouds that sweep across the summits. It is a mountain region that inspires awe in all who are privileged to see it.

For the mountaineer, the overpowering physical impact is heightened by the human story. The world's finest climbers have been irresistibly drawn to these mountains. Here they have played out some of the most dramatic ascents, and retreats, in the history of the sport. Who can gaze at Cerro Torre and not think of Toni Egger and Cesare Maestri? Two climbers, alone, attempting such a peak in 1958! This incredibly bold attempt is one of the most significant events in alpinism — regardless of whether or not they reached the summit.

Alan Kearney, like many before him, has fallen under the spell of these regions. He has given us here a rich reward. He has combined a thorough history of ascents of the major peaks with forceful accounts of his own climbs on these same peaks. From his pictures and personal experiences, we gain an intimate sense of these fabulous mountains. We gain as well an insight into the highest levels of alpinism by following Alan up demanding routes on three of the peaks. And from the history we too can visualize the great events, the storms, the bivouacs, the inevitable tragedies, the human drama which has unfolded — and continues to unfold — among these mountains.

Alan is certainly well qualified to write this story. He is not only a first-rate climber; he is imbued with deep feelings for this lovely region. He sees a present unimagined by the pioneers; Patagonia is becoming a victim to its own attractiveness. The solitude remarked upon by earlier visitors is largely gone. But go in winter, or travel away from the more popular trails, and you will still find the true Patagonia.

But Patagonia is not only the place Alan has so well described; it is a symbol of remoteness, of challenge, of the last, purest mountaineering. If it did not exist, we would have had to invent it. We have to believe in the impossible dream. Tomorrow's adventurers will need to seek their own Patagonias. They will do so, to continue the quest so admirably exemplified in these pages; the quest for the ultimate in commitment and difficulty.

San Francisco, March 1992

PREFACE

Patagonia first came to my attention in 1971; while at college I read an article on the Towers of Paine in the *American Alpine Journal*. Though just a novice mountaineer at the time, I vowed to become skilled enough to climb in Patagonia. Ten years later I reached the summit of the Central Tower of Paine. I was hooked; over the next seven years I made four more expeditions to Patagonia.

On these trips I photographed my climbs; later I wrote articles for magazines and journals. The region fascinated me; as my experiences grew so did my love for these mountains. Finding there was no collected record in print about mountaineering in Patagonia, I felt the need to record my ascents and those of other climbers in a book.

The peaks, mostly well under 4000 meters high, have attracted many of the world's leading climbers for over thirty years; including Lionel Terray, Don Whillans, José Luis Fonrouge, Yvon Chouinard and Reinhard Karl. The failures are many, the victories few and yet, in three decades, the visits have increased and the legends have grown. Patagonia produces some of the worst weather in the world, on the most inaccessible summits. Despite the wind, rain and snow, Patagonia has drawn climbers with incredible determination and brought forth the most bizarre equipment, some never used before or since. Climbers have tackled the sheer walls with gas powered air compressors for drilling bolts and worn neoprene skin diving suits.

Patagonia conveys different images. The nine letters compressed into a 16 × 45mm label represent a line of clothing to buyers of outdoor wear. Historians recall Butch Cassidy eluding the law, as he roamed the dry grasslands of southern Argentina. Biologists identify the name with the penguins, whales and seals that flourish off the Argentine coast. Sailors have visions of incredible storms that set ships on their beams. Potential trekkers are lured by color brochures filled with photographs of wild animals, tidewater glaciers and sheer mountains wrapped in gleaming ice. But to some of us, Patagonia is the home of three compact groups of tantalizing peaks that offer outstanding climbing. Within these pages are the stories of some of Patagonia's great climbs, and of those who have done them.

ACKNOWLEDGEMENTS

I would like to thank Roberta Lowe and Jill Neate for their encouragement, suggestions and the long hours they spent reviewing and editing this book. Dave Dailey, Talbot Bielefeldt, Jill Fugate and Ginger Oppenheimer looked over early drafts and provided helpful direction. A special thanks to Silvia Metzeltin and Gino Buscaini for furnishing route information, and for allowing Don Lowe to remake the maps from their originals.

Michael Bearzi supplied the striking photograph of Cerro Torre from the west, and Jennifer Hahn created the route topos that appear herein.

I thank with all my heart my close friend Bobby Knight and my wife Sue for their compassion and cooperation on our climbs together.

Finally, I am grateful to my parents for introducing me to the mountain environment 34 years ago; it was from them that I learned both artistic expression and wholesome alpine ethics.

FOREWORD

Although the Fitz Roy and Paine mountains are the focus of this book, there are many other peaks in Patagonia, which lie north to the Río Negro and west across the northern and southern Patagonian Ice Caps. In the north of the region, San Lorenzo, San Valentín and Cerro Castillo, among others, offer challenging snow and ice climbs at elevations between 2700 and 4100 meters.

The Fitz Roy and Paine mountains are 160 kilometers apart and are bordered on the west by the South Patagonian Ice Cap. All along this huge mass of continental ice are scores of peaks rising above a thick mantle of snow and ice. Forty-five kilometers northwest of Fitz Roy, the once mysterious Volcán Lautaro attains a height of 3379 meters. In 1964 an expedition of Argentine climbers ascended Lautaro; they found fumaroles and small craters in the sleeping volcano.

Because Patagonia contains so many mountains spread over such a large area, I have concentrated on the most spectacular peaks; Fitz Roy, Cerro Torre and the Towers of Paine. These have been the focus of climbing in Patagonia.

Climbs are dealt with chronologically within the chapters covering these peaks, but not every climb is covered. A full alphabetical list of peaks and climbs is given in Appendix II, together with brief route information. Those ascents described in detail were chosen for reasons that range from historical significance and route quality to the style of the first ascent. Climbs up a major unclimbed face are included, whereas variations on routes are often excluded. I tried to select climbs that contributed to an advancement in style or technique; and climbs that utilized unusual and sometimes revolutionary equipment. Several unsuccessful attempts could not be ignored because of the controversy surrounding them or because the face still awaits a complete ascent. By definition, a first ascent means the initial climb to the highest summit of a mountain by any route. A new route means the first ascent of an unclimbed ridge, buttress, couloir or face.

It is sometimes difficult to ascertain whether or not a climbing party reached the actual summit, based on what they have written in magazine and journal articles. Recently there has been a trend

13

toward claiming first ascents or new routes when the climb ended below the summit, a new route is not carried through to the summit or the new route ends where it joins an established route. These assertions are unacceptable; the Italian climber-writer Silvia Metzeltin explains why. "In Patagonia the greatest difficulties do not always lie in the technical problems, but more often in the hostile climate that surrounds the peaks; the last few meters in Patagonia, even if they are the easiest, are part of the whole. There, luck with the weather is part of the game and whoever doesn't like it should go somewhere else."

So famous are the ice capped spires that, in a slide lecture about Mount Everest, Ned Gillette referred to a cluster of snow formations as, "Patagonia-like ice mushrooms." Even those with many high standard climbs under their belts speak reverently of the rime plastered granite walls of Fitz Roy and Cerro Torre. Yvon Chouinard certainly had in mind Patagonia when he wrote, more than twenty years ago, "The future of Yosemite Valley will be as a training ground for a new generation of super alpinists who will venture forth to the high mountains of the world to do the most aesthetic and difficult walls on the face of the earth." The most aesthetic and difficult walls lie in Alaska, the Himalaya and Patagonia; a new generation of alpinists has been hard at work in these regions since Chouinard's comment.

The entire region called Patagonia extends 1770 kilometers, from the Strait of Magellan at the southernmost tip of the South American mainland north to the Río Negro; it is bordered by the Pacific Ocean to the west and the Atlantic Ocean to the east.

Fitz Roy and Cerro Torre lie in the southern part of Patagonia and are 410 kilometers north-northwest of the Strait of Magellan. To the east, the rugged peaks are flanked by 290 kilometers of dry Argentine pampas. Westward, barely 48 kilometers of continental ice separate the mountains from the Chilean fjords snaking inland from the Pacific Ocean. Southeast of Fitz Roy and Cerro Torre, Lago Viedma and Lago Argentino collect the snowmelt in two natural reservoirs 72 and 96 kilometers in length. The icy waters are carried to the Atlantic Ocean via the Río Santa Cruz.

The Paine mountains (pronounced *Pie-knee*) are 265 kilometers northwest of the Strait of Magellan, and are virtually the same distance from the Chilean fjords and the Atlantic as is Fitz Roy. Melting snow and ice drain into Lago Nordenskjöld, Lago Pehoe and Lago Sarmiento to the south. Waters from these three lakes travel to the Pacific Ocean via the Río Serrano and Seno Ultima Esperanza.

To gain a better perspective on what Patagonia is like today, it is necessary to go back nearly five centuries, to the time when Europeans first visited the southernmost shores of South America.

In 1520 the Portugese explorer Ferdinand Magellan sailed around the world in search of a shorter route to the spices and silks of India and the Far East. In his book, *In Patagonia,* Bruce Chatwin credits Magellan with giving Patagonia its name. Through research, Chatwin surmised that Magellan had been reading a fictional story involving a beast called the Grand Patagon. When Magellan stepped ashore to winter over at San Julian, he was greeted by a giant Indian dancing on the sand. Because the Indian was clothed in guanaco skins, with his face and hair painted red, white and yellow, Magellan associated him with the beast in the book. The small European responded, "Ha! Patagon!" Thus Patagonia became the land of the Patagon.

The Indians that Magellan encountered came from northern South America around 9500 BC. The early natives wandered south, following game along the fringes of the Andes mountains. The Tehuelches, who greeted Magellan, and the Onas became nomadic hunters of the plains. The Chonos, Alacalufs and Yahgans inhabited the coastal waterways and gathered seafood. From archeological evidence, it is known that some remaining Ice Age mammals co-existed with these early peoples. Mylodons (giant ground sloths), glyptodons (large armadillos) and camelids, such as the guanaco, munched on the tough grasses and small green leaves of the Magellan beech tree. Eventually, climatic changes brought on droughts that reduced the forage on which the big mammals relied in order to survive. Cataclysmic events, in the form of volcanic eruptions, earth quakes and floods, killed many other animals in a land where the earth's crust moves frequently. As new species of animals migrated from the north, disease and competition further reduced the populations of indigenous mammals.

Like the animals, the native peoples suffered from intruders. Imported diseases claimed the lives of Indians, as did the battles fought over land disputes. Barbed wire fences for containing sheep thwarted the Indians' nomadic existence and their numbers dwindled, as had the pre-historic beasts before them.

In 1578 the Englishman Sir Francis Drake sought the riches of the east, as Magellan had done. The superstitious Drake claimed the natives were responsible for the terrible weather near Cape Horn. He later wrote how they created the storms. "They built great fires and then cast upon them heaps of sand, as a sacrifice to the devils." Of Drake's three ships, only his, the *Golden Hind,* made it through to the Pacific Ocean. Following Drake's voyage, Europeans began to settle Patagonia. In 1584 Spain attempted to colonize southern Patagonia, in hopes of protecting the coasts of Chile and Peru from pirates. However, there were neither adequate foodstuffs nor tools to construct proper shelters; 350 Spanish settlers died during the first winter. The site was later appropriately named Port Famine. Shipwrecked mariners added their own labels to the barren and stormy region; on modern maps names such as Desolation Island and Useless Bay stand out.

The Dutch captain Wilhelm Schouten completed the first true rounding of the tip of Cape Horn in 1616. Schouten named the cape for his home town of Hoorn. One of his two ships hit a narwhal and, while beached for repairs, the ship caught fire and burned to the ground. These incidents reinforced rumors and beliefs that the region of Cape Horn was a cursed land, but they did not slow the increasing stream of men and ships sailing south.

From 1681 to 1720 pirates utilized the maze of channels for refuge and a base from which to raid passing ships. In the late eighteenth century, more attempts to colonize the coastline failed. Philip Parker King and Robert Fitz Roy, who captained British ships, charted the waters and shore for almost ten years, beginning in 1826. On one of the voyages of Fitz Roy's *Beagle,* Charles Darwin made observations in Patagonia that contributed to his theory of natural selection. In 1843 Chileans established a colony near present day Punta Arenas, to control the waterways used by ships on a regular basis; eventually it became a major port for shipping wool, mutton and beef from the eastern Patagonia grasslands. Permanent cities made Patagonia increasingly attractive to potential immigrants; during the period 1879-83 the plains were settled by Spaniards, Yugoslavs, Arabs, Germans, Poles, Rumanians and the British, including a distinctive Welsh community.

By 1974 more than one million people inhabited Chilean and Argentine Patagonia. Livelihoods ranged from the raising of sheep and cattle to mining, fishing, tourism and oil production. The sheep population had been as high as twenty million but the guanacos, competing for the same forage, declined rapidly. The Los Glaciares (Fitz Roy) and Torres del Paine national parks now exclude sheep grazing and the guanaco population is growing larger. At present, there are an estimated 2000 guanacos in the Paine Park.

Although estancias, which support livestock, exist at the western edge of the pampas, very few people live in the two mountain regions discussed in this book. Part of the reason lies in topography; the mountains rise abruptly from the dry flat grasslands, leaving only a very small foothill zone that can support habitation. The few residents are immigrants who usurped the land from the natives. A climbing expedition might enlist a gaucho and his horses to move gear to base camp and possibly bump into one or two horse guides leading tourists in for a view. Patagonia lacks the mountain cultures that exist in Bolivia, Peru, Ecuador, Nepal, Tibet and Pakistan. The Italian climber Silvia Metzeltin feels the absence of culture is beneficial. "Patagonia is a good place for adventure. There are only mountaineers and nature."

16

Foreword

Pictures have always exerted a powerful force on climbers. In 1949, the Italian missionary, Father Alberto De Agostini, brought out a very fine Italian edition of his book, ***Ande Patagoniche,*** which illustrated the major mountains of Patagonia with black and white photographs. His mountaineering countrymen, excited by the scores of unclimbed peaks, organized an expedition to Fitz Roy the following year. Between 1937 and 1967, climbing activity in Patagonia was sporadic. Interest in Patagonia grew after the third ascent of Fitz Roy in 1968 and the general surge of climbing activity throughout the world in the early 1970's. Since then, climbers have come regularly to Patagonia from all over the globe. In 1988, American, Argentine, Austrian, Italian, Polish, Norwegian and Spanish climbers were simultaneously camped below Cerro Torre, waiting for good weather. The region's popularity has increased with the help of films, articles and lectures, as successive waves of climbers have turned to Patagonia to test their skills on the wind hammered spires.

1

MOUNTAINS, GLACIERS AND WEATHER:
An overview of the natural forces at work
in the Fitz Roy, Cerro Torre and Paine massifs

Formation of the mountains

Hundreds of millions of years before mountaineers began to explore Patagonia, South America and Africa formed a super-continent. The mechanisms that move land masses, and which transported South America to where it is today, lie beneath the surface of the earth. This theory of continental drift is now commonly accepted by scientists and it is the subduction zone (where crustal plates collide) that has created that portion of the Andes where there are seventy-five mountains over 6000 meters. This zone, between the Nazca Plate (in the Pacific Ocean) and the South American Plate (including the continent and the southwestern Atlantic Ocean), tapers off just north of the Fitz Roy and Paine massifs. Had the subduction zone extended further south, the Fitz Roy and Paine mountains might have been much higher and larger.

Even in the subduction zone, where activity was greatest, much of the molten rock that rose upwards never reached the surface. The rock cooled and subsided 600 to 900 meters below and, in the case of Fitz Roy and the Paine, crystallized to form the huge intrusion known as the Patagonian Batholith. The surrounding rocks eroded and weathered away leaving the batholiths exposed. In the Paine group, many of the peaks are capped by black slate. These older sedimentary rocks were pushed up as the batholith rose and are especially pronounced on the summits of the Cuernos (horns) del Paine. The black caps on the Cuernos, Fortress and Shield are known as "roof pendants" because they are the remnants of a huge sedimentary roof. Earlier intrusions took place between the Jurassic and Cretaceous geologic periods 135 million years ago; later intrusions in the Tertiary, roughly ten to sixty million years ago.

Granites generally constitute a small percentage of the intrusive bodies in the entire Andean range but, especially from 45 degrees south latitude to Tierra Del Fuego, there are extensive masses of plutonic rocks. The granitic rocks in the Paine group are composed primarily of quartz monzonites with transitions to biotite and olivine monzonites. Quartz diorite makes up the lower portions of the Fortress and the three principal Towers of Paine. The grey diorite is not as solid as the yellow-orange quartz monzonite that characterizes the towers when viewed from afar. For comparison, quartz monzonite is of the same type as the rock found in Joshua Tree National Monument, California.

Fifty million years from now, erosion may have completely wiped out the magnificent granite spires and the crustal plates, if they move at the present rate, will have shifted thousands of kilometers. South America will creep west to collide with the Phillipines and Japan. Should this occur, the mountains, climate and glaciers of Patagonia today will change drastically.

Ice ages and glaciers

A continent situated near the equator has a much different climate from one positioned near the poles. Continental drift shifted land masses into the higher latitudes and, as a result, temperatures dropped in those areas. The movement of land masses could have induced three major glacial ages during the earth's history. These ice ages occurred in the Pre-Cambrian Era, 700 million years ago; the Permo-Carboniferous, 300 million years ago; and the late Cenozoic, ten million years ago.

The onset of an ice age, with its attendant continental ice caps and glaciers, is directly related to solar energy which is either absorbed or reflected by the earth. As the earth shifts slightly on its axis from season to season, there is a change in the angle that the sun strikes the surface of the earth, and thus a change in temperature. At the low latitudes nearer the equator, the earth heats up; nearer the poles it cools down.

The degree of growth of an ice cap or glacier depends on how much snow falls each year and how much melts and evaporates. Climatic changes cause glaciers to grow or shrink; it is also thought that astronomic variations or changes in orbital eccentricity could have produced the ice ages by a shift in the geographical and seasonal distribution of sunlight. The last series of glacial advances and retreats was during the Pleistocene epoch, which began 1.8 million years ago.

During this time the great ice sheets carved away masses of granite from the Patagonian Batholith. Phenomenal spires were created in places where the rock had intruded higher, was harder and more resistant, or where the volume of ice had more cutting power. On the plains east of the Patagonian Andes, the ice spread out to a distance of 200 kilometers. This was the maximum expansion attained 18,000 years ago; the ice, without moisture to feed it, could advance no further under the rain shadow of the high mountains. To the west the spreading glacier ice was stopped by deep water, where it probably formed a narrow floating shelf that calved continually into the sea. Only in the Strait of Magellan did Argentine Patagonian ice reach seawater. The extensive ice sheets disappeared 10,000 years ago and the smaller glaciers that remain are in retreat. Typical of the area is the Paine's Dickson Glacier, which is backing up nearly eighteen meters per year.

Although the present day Hielo Continental (continental ice cap) was originally much larger, it has persisted due to geographic location, elevation and moisture. Because the tip of South America is nearer to Antarctica than the other continents (Cape Horn is barely 640 kilometers from the Palmer Peninsula) it is subjected to the cold currents flowing northwards, especially the Humboldt Current. The land mass is 900 to 1500 meters above the sea, most of the moisture it receives is in the form of snow. Both geographical position and ocean currents make the Hielo Continental closer to the equator by nearly 1600 kilometers when compared to Alaskan and Norwegian counterparts of similar size. Glaciologist Otto Nordenskjöld wrote about the ice age in 1928. "Glaciers covered large areas in southern Patagonia, whose mountain regions in modern times are more heavily ice covered than any other tract so far from the poles."

Glacier Moreno is a very active, 35 kilometer long valley glacier that flows off the Patagonian Ice Cap between the Paine and Fitz Roy massifs. Every three to four years, Moreno advances against a slab of solid rock between Lago Argentino and one of its western arms, Brazo Rico. Brazo Rico, together with Brazo Sur (with a combined area of 207 square kilometers), must empty into Lago Argentino by flowing past the snout of Glacier Moreno. But Moreno's sixty meter high wall of ice blocks the emptying waters and the two sheets of water rise against the natural ice dam. In 1988 the lakes rose 36 meters above their normal level before the tremendous weight of the water began to undermine the dam. A tunnel formed beneath the snout and the frothing mass of exiting water plucked huge pieces of ice from the glacier and carried them downstream. As the dam was further weakened, sixty meter high séracs fell into the newly formed river. Brazo Rico and Brazo Sur had taken months to fill behind the dam, yet they emptied to their former levels in just a few days.

Localized climate might cause Moreno's continual advance and thus the dam to form. Greater snowfall and colder temperatures occurring in that area could create a situation where accumulation exceeds ablation and Moreno grows. Present advances also reflect the time lag between climatic effects and the glaciers reaction to them.

At the northernmost end of the ice cap, the San Rafaél Glacier calves ice into the sea from a wall forty to sixty meters high. San Rafaél is the only glacier in the world so close to the equator that reaches the sea. This remarkable ice sheet has a profound effect upon the weather that batters the Fitz Roy and Paine areas.

Climate and weather

The ice cap is actually divided into two ice caps; the northern one is 120 kilometers long and the southern 380 kilometers long. Together they have a surface area of 23,300 square kilometers (the size of Vermont) and it is the Southern Patagonian Ice Cap that is primarily responsible for the climate in the Fitz Roy, Cerro Torre and Paine regions. To understand what is occurring over the ice cap, it is necessary to examine the atmospheric conditions between the latitudes of 30 degrees and 65 degrees south.

Temperature decreases rapidly toward the South Pole and this area is referred to as a transition zone between tropical and subtropical warm air and the polar cold air. This Planetary Frontal Zone occurs in both hemispheres but produces lower temperatures in South America due to the proximity to Antarctica and the Humboldt Current. Midsummer temperatures at Los Evangelistas Island (52 degrees south) in southern Chile are comparable to the midwinter temperatures at Valentia (52 degrees north) in southwest Ireland. Strong west winds characterize the zone in which giant waves and vortices form from differential heating and physical deflection by high mountains and plateaus.

The westerly sea air carries moisture that cools down as it moves across the ice cap. Waves and vortices create a meeting of winds from different directions, forming a convergence zone. Areas of low pressure and convergence zones result in thick clouds and precipitation. As the air masses meet, they rise, cool and then condense. Rain and snow often arrive in large amounts (750 centimeters annually). Rime ice is also common and forms on the windward side of objects. Supercooled fog particles come in contact with surfaces, at temperatures below freezing point, giving the rocky summits a crenelated appearance.

Wind and precipitation spell trouble for the alpinist and he learns to identify an oncoming storm by the types of clouds forming. Generally speaking, any clouds approaching the mountains from the ice cap, that have been compressed or stretched by the wind, indicate the arrival of a major storm. Special types of clouds called lee waves form on the downwind sides of mountains. A wave pattern forms and the initial trough may then be followed by an alternate series of crests and troughs of decreasing height. The length of the wave depends on the wind speed and the height depends on the shape of the mountain. Lee waves are indicated by the presence of characteristic clouds that form in the crest of the wave. Thin arched clouds and lens shaped clouds are most common and when thin arched clouds are stacked one above the other they are referred to as a "une pile d'assiettes" (pile of plates). It is thought that these clouds are created by air mixing, which produces alternately humid and dry layers. In Patagonia, extremely long, thin clouds are common. They are usually the result of unevaporated ice particles at the downwind edge of a wave cloud. All of these clouds owe their streamlined shapes to the wind.

South America's tip is a narrow strip of land that forms a weak barrier to moving air currents, so wind speeds tend to be constant. Los Evangelistas Island has recorded gale force winds (79 kilometers per hour) on eighty days in one year. In Greenland and Antarctica, extreme winds occur for the same reasons as in Patagonia. All three areas have smooth ice caps which offer no resistance to the passing wind. The mountains cause the wind to gain momentum; climbers have found cols and passes particularly vile places to meet the onrushing foe.

Apart from mountain topography and the smooth surface of the ice, the ice cap may be responsible for katabatic (downslope) winds in the Fitz Roy and Paine mountains. Air flows off the ice cap and down into the valleys where the granite spires rise out of the eastern edge of the Hielo Continental. However, the weather is not always bad; the Argentine climber José Luis Fonrouge (who made the second ascent of Fitz Roy) has a tip for identifying good weather. "Good weather is coming if the Argentine flag is pointing north and the condor is flying low in circles." On a summer day, air that is heated by contact with hot ground, rises and these columns of air called thermals are sought by the great birds. Today, the causes of weather are known but scientists and mountaineers cannot manipulate it any more than the local peoples. In his book, **Land of Tempest,** the renowned mountain explorer Eric Shipton described some of the native superstitions concerning weather.

"The Alacaluf Indians believed that bad weather is caused by throwing sand or pebbles at a hut or into the water; by killing a parrot or even looking at a flock flying overhead, and when shellfish are eaten on a voyage, the shells must be kept until they can be deposited on land, well above the high water mark."

Modern climbers tend to be superstitious in their own way and especially about Patagonian weather. John Bragg who, with two other Americans, made the first ascent of Torre Egger in 1976, felt lucky when they were able to climb for two days in a row. "Maybe if we are very quiet, we may slip by undetected for two or three days. The weather god down there is no fool. It's hard to climb unnoticed for long. Sooner or later, usually sooner, he creeps in like an unwanted guest. Tipped off by a shout of, 'Off belay!'"

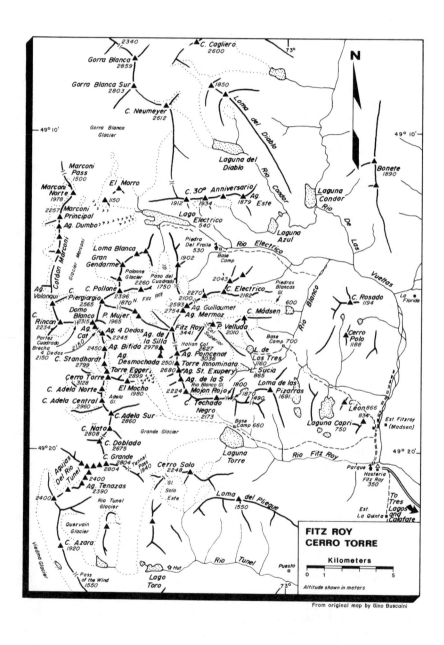

2

THE FITZ ROY GROUP

Fitz Roy, at 3441 meters, is the dominant mountain on a ridge of peaks and spires that lies on a north to south axis. Aguja Guillaumet (2539 meters) and Aguja Mermoz (2754 meters) are small, blocky granite peaks to the north, that form a foundation for the skyscraper of Fitz Roy. Three slender structures lie to the south of Fitz Roy, respectively Aguja Poincenot (3036 meters), Aguja Rafaél (2501 meters) and Aguja St. Exupéry (2680 meters). On the southwest flank of Fitz Roy are two gendarmes (Desmochada and Aguja de la Silla) that have only recently been climbed. To better comprehend the size of Fitz Roy, one should realize that the barely discernible spire of Desmochada produced a climb fifteen pitches long. Although these pages cover only the major climbs on Fitz Roy and Poincenot, many quality ascents have been done on these smaller peaks. Guillaumet, Mermoz and St. Exupéry were named after 1930's pilots who flew the Patagonia mail.

Three main glaciers continue to carve away the hard granite of Fitz Roy. On the northwest side, the Fitz Roy Glacier drains into Lago Eléctrico which supplies silt choked water to the Río Eléctrico. The Piedras Blancas Glacier steadily chews on the eastern walls of the mountain and feeds its snow and ice melt into the Río Blanco. On the southwest slopes of Fitz Roy, the sinuous Torre Glacier merges with Glacier Grande. Meltwater from both rivers of ice sustains Lago Torre and the Río Fitz Roy. Above the Torre Glacier and between Aguja de la Silla and the Italian Col, sits a small hanging glacier at the top of a huge gully.

Early exploration

In 1782 Antonio Viedma led an expedition for the Spanish government to establish settlements and to explore the waterways of Patagonia. Guided by Tehuelche Indians, Viedma followed the Río Chalia southwest to the large lake that today bears his name. From the northern shore of the lake, Viedma described two great mountains, "Their sharp cones dominate all other mountains. The Indians call them 'Chalten'." Because of the wind driven plume of clouds and snow around the summit of the higher peak, the natives thought it was an active volcano. From 1826 onwards, the British captains Phillip Parker King and Robert Fitz Roy sailed ships to Patagonia as part of a quest to South America. In 1831 Fitz Roy, Charles Darwin and a small crew rowed three whaling boats 290 kilometers up the Río Santa Cruz. They failed to reach Lago Argentino but succeeded in getting a glimpse of Chalten. Near the end of the nineteenth century, Argentine geographer Francisco Moreno led a mission to accurately determine the border between Chile and Argentina. Moreno and his men fought their way in small boats up the Río Santa Cruz to Lago Viedma,then travelled on horseback to the base of Chalten. He named a number of peaks in the area, the greatest of them for Robert Fitz Roy.

On an expedition in 1902 Rodolfo Hauthal noted that Fitz Roy was composed of granitic rock, not a volcano as the Indians had believed. Hauthal's principal objective was to study the area's geology and glaciation; in that he was successful. The first climbing in the area occurred in 1916 when the Argentines Lutz Witte, Fritz Kühn and Alfredo Kölliker probed the valley of the Rio Tunel and climbed Cerro Huemul (2750m) which lies eighteen kilometers due south of Fitz Roy.

In 1930 Father Alberto De Agostini made geographical observations of the watershed around Fitz Roy with Everisto Croux and Leon Bron. The following year, with Mario Derriard, he explored the glaciated areas west of Lago Viedma. Growing increasingly fascinated with Fitz Roy, De Agostini organized a small expedition in 1935 to explore the flanks of the mountain. Accompanied by professional Italian alpine guides from Courmayeur, Louis Carrel and Joseph Pellissier, he climbed to a high point northeast of Fitz Roy and named the peak Cerro Eléctrico.

Two years later, climbers from Italy, including Count Aldo Bonacossa, Ettore Castiglione, GB Gilberti and Leo Dubosc, attempted Fitz Roy and reached the saddle between Poincenot and Fitz Roy's South Ridge. For the first time, climbers had actually set foot on the mountain; the Italians' high point now bears the name *Brecha de los Italianos, The Italian Col.* This is the same route by which French climbers in 1952, and many subsequent expeditions, gained access to the difficult upper walls of the mountain.

Although Fitz Roy appeared to offer no weaknesses, the attempts became more frequent. In 1948 the Argentine Hans Zechner, with Mario Bertone and N Gianolini, tried to climb a large couloir on the southwest side, between Desmochada and Poincenot. After seven hours of climbing in the gully and bombardment from falling stones, they retreated. Failing there, Zechner attempted the lower buttress of the mountain's northern ridge and made a third attempt from the Eléctrico side. One year later Zechner put in a final effort by climbing part way up the north spur and ridge. This feature he named *Mannequin's Crest,* a nightmarish ridge of gendarmes and overhanging walls that constitute Val de Biois, Mermoz and Guillaumet. With its vertical rock, often coated in ice and lashed by wind and snow, the monolith seemed insurmountable to the climbers of the day.

First ascent of Fitz Roy: 1952

By the 1940's French climbers had become a leading force in the world of alpinism, completing many first ascents in the Alps and abroad. In 1950 a team of French climbers scaled Annapurna (8090 meters) in Nepal. This was the first eight thousand meter peak to be climbed; it was technically more difficult than the ascent of Everest three years later. A team of French climbers, led by Dr. M A Azema, began organizing an expedition to climb Fitz Roy in 1951. Azema was an avid climber and frequently practiced on the steep limestone cliffs of the southern Cevennes. He was familiar with Fitz Roy and in his book, *The Conquest of Fitz Roy*, Azema later recalled his fascination with the mountain. "I had retained from childhood a vivid memory of Darwin's *Voyage of the Beagle*, combined with Jules Verne's stories of the Magellan Archipelago. And a picture had formed in my mind of an astonishing mountain soaring up not far from Cape Horn and appearing through rents in the cloud wrack like a vision from Edgar Allen Poe."

Non-climbers often believe that only the highest mountains are difficult. Altitude is not the only measure by which a hard ascent is judged. In the Himalaya the climber is battling with thin air, bad weather, dangerous icefalls and faces of tremendous scale. In Patagonia the fight to reach the top is governed by three elements; bad weather, difficult climbing and huge walls. In general, the Himalaya contain many peaks with at least one route that has technically easy to moderate climbing. But in Patagonia all the major peaks are more technically difficult. This is not to say that any one range is the ultimate challenge on earth. What Patagonia lacks in lung wrenching thin air, it makes up for with desperate maneuvers on iced up rock. A Himalayan peak may have gentle snow slopes that require little knowledge of climbing technique, but which take hours or even days to ascend in the oxygen starved air. The French had to explain all these points to interested supporters of their expedition.

They pointed out that a mountain of such difficulty (although only 3441 meters high) had never been attempted before. Of the world's great summits, few were guarded on every side by smooth, vertical rock. Without financial help the team could not hope to reach the mountain they so desperately wanted to climb. With the enlistment and assistance of Réné Ferlet (Secretary of the Club

Alpin Francais) and Georges Strouve, the expedition received the recognition and monetary support of the Himalayan Committee and of the Alpine Club.

Climbing in the early 1950's was much more of a novelty than it is now. When the group arrived in Buenos Aires they became celebrities, fêted at luncheons and cocktail parties. Argentine President Juan Perón met the team and promised them assistance in reaching the mountain. In Argentina, the French climbers Louis Depasse and L Lliboutry (a scientist as well) joined the expedition and the Argentine Lieutenant Francisco Ibañez became their Liaison Officer.

An Argentine expedition to Pier Giorgio, led by Gerhardt Watzl, met the French climbers and took them climbing at a nearby abandoned factory, a precursor to modern day artificial climbing walls. Jean Pillet was a French medical student living in Argentina and a member of the 1951-52 Pier Giorgio expedition. On a previous trip to France, Pillet had been to a friend's house that had been bombed during the Second World War and did some climbing on the brick walls. He said, "This gave me the idea back in Buenos Aires I knew where a factory was in ruins; and sometimes I like to climb this factory. This gave way to a generation of good (Argentine) climbers." The French expedition to Fitz Roy and the Argentine expedition to Pier Giorgio planned to be in the mountains during the same period but would not share the same base camp or interact with each other.

President Perón arranged for two army trucks to transport all their gear from Santa Cruz to the road end at Estancia Madsen. The group had brought only selected lightweight foods from France and, of course, their own Burgundy wine. Much more was needed to supply their six week attack on the mountain; Azema describes a shopping spree in Santa Cruz. "Ferlet and Depasse ordered whole cases of *cabaja,* a big oily fish from La Plata, sardines, corned beef, frankfurter sausages, canned and dried fruit, jam, sugar, honey, cake, *criolitas,* salted biscuits, sweet biscuits, tinned vegetables, cheeses, hams, enormous Bologna sausages, olive oil in cans. Lionel must have infected the party with his own remarkable appetite, or had he secretly decided to climb every peak in Patagonia?"

On 24 and 25 December the loaded trucks bumped along the 370 kilometers of dirt road from Santa Cruz to the confluence of the Río Fitz Roy and Río Las Vueltes, sixteen kilometers from Fitz Roy. The arid grasslands of the pampas were alive with wild animals. Guanacos, *maras* (a large hare), ñandús (the South American ostrich) and hairy armadillos could be observed running away from the noisy vehicles. Occasionally another two legged creature exercised its leg muscles; Terray, bored with inactivity and tired of eating dust, leaped to the ground, tore off his shirt, and sprinted along the edge of the road.

At the end of the road, Fitz Roy's kilometer-and-a-half high grey granite walls rose above the rolling carpets of green beech forests and the untrodden summit glistened beneath a blue sky. Here the climbers unloaded the trucks and began sorting the piles of equipment into loads appropriate for horses to carry. Terray shot a hare for dinner and roasted it over a brushwood fire. Already the taste of canned foods had lost their appeal and the group welcomed fresh meat. The local estancia owner, Andreas Madsen, offered his hospitality to the Frenchmen and provided horses for hire. Madsen had witnessed five expeditions to Fitz Roy fail to climb the peak and was skeptical as to whether the newcomers could do any better. Azema explained to Madsen that techniques and equipment had improved in recent years; that those with him were very skilled and determined climbers.

In 1952 no bridge spanned the Río Fitz Roy; the river, swollen by spring snow melt, was a major obstacle. Terray and Poincenot selected a reasonable place to ford the glacier fed stream, then Terray fixed a line from one bank to the other to safeguard their crossing. Poincenot clipped himself into the rope with a carabiner and started across. He lost his footing, the current quickly drew him under. The rope, anchored to a rucksack full of stones on one bank, broke loose; Poincenot slid to the knotted end and drowned.

Grieved by the loss of their comrade, the expedition nevertheless pushed forward. Two separate teams investigated the mountain; one from the Río Eléctrico Valley, the other from the Río Blanco side. Like the Italians in 1937, the French eventually chose to attack the peak from the Río Blanco, up to Lago Los Tres, up the Los Tres Glacier to Col Superior and then across the Piedras Glacier to the couloir below the Italian Col. Every face rose between 1500 and 2400 meters except for the east face below the Italian Col and the south spur. That face and spur gained 940 meters above the Piedras Glacier and appeared the most feasible line to the French in 1952.

For two weeks, they ferried gear and food to the couloir beneath the Italian Col, between short intense storms that dumped a meter of snow. While half the group brought up loads, the other half began climbing and fixing ropes up the snow, ice and mixed ground. By 22 January a small cave had been hacked out of hard snow and ice on the east side of the slope above the Col. After dumping their gear, Terray and Magnone explored the route above. The pair struggled all afternoon on smooth, nearly holdless rock, gaining only one rope length. The wind picked up as they rappelled down to the snow. With few supplies remaining in the cave, it was impossible to wait out the storm.

The entire expedition regrouped in the comfort of a log hut nestled amid Magellan beech trees. At an elevation of 760 meters the temperature was milder and the raging wind less powerful than up at the Col. Nevertheless, treetops swayed violently as the boulders groaned beneath their roots; wave after wave of air blasts roared down the mountainside and across the forest. The sounds of a Patagonian storm are terrifying and eerie. Terray and his companions hoped the storm would be a short one.

The subject of weather was a constant topic, Terray voiced his opinion. "At Chamonix it (the route) would be in the bag. But here it all depends on the wind." When they asked Madsen if they could expect any more calm, clear spells of weather, he replied, "Days of fine weather? Well, yes, there are some. Several every summer. You've already had a good many. More than other summers. You mustn't complain."

Terray maintained his mental energy through the long storms and shouted life into the other seven climbers on the morning of 30 January, when the skies cleared. The team carried enough food and fuel up to the 2743 meter Italian Col to support a long siege on the mountain. Half a ton of ropes, hardware, clothing, sleeping bags, cook pots and cameras filled every corner of the snow cave, including a five kilo ham. Magnone and Terray felt the strongest, they left the cave at dawn on the following day intent on climbing and fixing 120 meters of rope. This would give them an edge when the summit attempt became feasible. All day they hammered in pitons for direct aid and clawed their way up ice lined cracks. One such fissure was too wide to wedge hands and feet inside but too narrow to accept the climber's body. Terray climbed the crack by jamming with his elbows and the toes and heels of his boots.

Strenuous climbing, made slippery by ice and snow, kept the two alpinists keyed up. Often a crack that looked surmountable repulsed their efforts and they would retreat and try again. As there was no guidebook, other climbers to consult or a line of debris from previous ascents to follow, Terray and Magnone relied on their experience and intuition. Such is the nature of forging a new route up a mountain. They returned to the cave that evening in fine weather and began organizing the equipment needed for a summit climb the following day. Above the fixed ropes, the pair estimated two days' climbing to the top, with one bivouac. They packed in rucksacks: one 60 meter 30mm (!) nylon rope; one 40 meter lighter nylon rope; wooden wedges; a number of steel and duralumin pitons; five three-runged stirrups; a score of aluminum carabiners; two **Marteau piolets** (north wall hammers); two sleeping bags of eider down and rubberized nylon; one 2 oz cake each; 2 oz of concentrated honey and nougat each; and glucose tablets containing a heart stimulant.

While the French expedition prepared to make their final bid with state of the art climbing equipment, the Argentines struggled to climb Pier Giorgio using homemade gear and plastic supermarket bags for rain clothing. Jean Pillet described his equipment. "We had carabiners made by an Austrian blacksmith in Buenos Aires and crampons also. The first real carabiners were given to us by Terray." Although the Argentines failed to climb Pier Giorgio (during the same period that Terray and Magnone went back up on Fitz Roy), they succeeded in making the first ascents of Domo Blanco and Cerro Marconi Norte, snowy peaks to the south and northwest respectively from Pier Giorgio.

The first of February was an exceptional day on Fitz Roy; not a breath of wind stirred, not a trace of cloud marred the sky. On the granite face each crystal and patch of ice sparkled in the morning sun. Magnone and Terray inhaled the sharp mountain air and felt energy surge through their stiff joints and sore muscles. An unclimbed summit lay above, in two days they hoped to reach it.

Climbing above the high point became more difficult with every rope length. Magnone, more experienced at direct aid climbing, led a delicate traverse into a crack, using some tension from a tenuous piton above him. After following the lead, Terray pulled out the piton with his thumb and forefinger. Terray climbed free up corners, over loose flakes and through chimneys, constantly having to clear ice away before driving in pitons. For fourteen hours the two alpinists struggled upward. Just before dark they found a gully filled with blocks, the only suitable bivouac site in 240 meters of climbing.

Settling in for the night, they were looking forward to a drink of water and a bite to eat but discovered that someone had packed metal flasks filled with stove fuel instead of water. They ate pieces of cake mixed with snow and squirmed for comfort on the uneven slope. Through the night the stars, instead of growing brighter, became dimmer behind a gauze of clouds. By morning a layer of black clouds grazed the pampas. The wind would surely arrive soon and obliterate the French team's chances of reaching the top.

A breeze caused their clothing to flutter, each had his doubts and secret fears. "Three fine days already. It can't last," Terray thought to himself. To lighten their load, he and Magnone took only one pack and no sleeping bags. It was time to start climbing. With weary eyes they picked out a line up the wall between blank rock on the left and overhanging cracks and ceilings on the right. The climbing was harder than ever and the malleable pitons, by nature, were difficult for the second man to remove. Their supply of anchors dwindled as more and more pitons could not be retrieved. Saucer shaped

31

clouds presaging a storm appeared. They estimated it would be tough to reach the summit before the storm hit. Without any pitons for protection, Magnone led a pitch over icy slabs and short overhangs. Terray, apprehensive about the difficulties and approaching storm, was for going down. Magnone had not been on many big expedition climbs before and did not know defeat. He asked Terray to allow him two more hours to push the route. A steep corner and couloir beckoned them higher and it looked as though the gentle snowfield leading to the summit was only a few meters away.

Magnone reached up to place one of the two remaining pitons for direct aid but it fell out of the crack as he touched it with the hammer. The other piton was too large for the tiny crack and he exclaimed that he needed an *ace of hearts* piton. The nearest one they could remember was fixed ninety meters below; impossible to recover at that late hour. Seeing no other route up, Magnone accepted defeat. But Terray scratched his head and said, "Guido, the sardine tin!" Guido looked up. Had Lionel gone mad? That sort of thing happened at 23,000 feet but at 10,000 feet? Lionel fumbled hastily in his sack, explaining, "You remember that tin of sardines, yesterday on the triangular snowpatch? I opened it with an *ace of hearts* which I think I put back in my sack, in the inner pocket. It must be there." Lionel pulled his things out, plunged his hand in and felt around. Then he gave a yell of triumph, "Here it is!"

---

1. Poincenot and Fitz Roy at dawn from Col Superior. This view from the east shows the first ascent route on Fitz Roy. The route climbed by the French in 1952 lies just right of the left skyline. Casarotto's 1979 North Pillar route is on the right skyline. The second ascent was by Bobby Knight and the author in 1984. *Nikon FM, 20mm lens, Kodachrome 64*

2. Fitz Roy at night and climber's headlight. After our snow cave melted, we slept in the open at Col Superior. We spent two days resting at the Col after our climb of the North Pillar. *Nikon FM, 20mm lens, K 64*

3. East Face of Poincenot from Rio Bravo basecamp. The 1962 first ascent route followed the diagonal snowy ramp up and left, then up the left-hand skyline. *Nikon F2, 600mm lens, K 64*

4. Climber on Torre Innominata and the North Face of Saint Exupery. While repeating the 1974 route on Innominata, we picked out an unclimbed line on nearby Saint Exupery. *Nikon FM, 20mm lens, K 64*

The small piece of steel, no heavier than a penknife and worth only a few francs, was the key to attaining the summit. Magnone pounded it in, stood up, and heaved himself across the east face to the snowfield. In half an hour the jubilant climbers set foot on the topmost boulders, as dense clouds from the developing storm enveloped them. Terray dug through his pockets and produced a Cassin carabiner. They heaped boulders over it as proof of their ascent and gave each other a hug.

By their first ascent of Fitz Roy, the French proved that difficult and beautiful mountains need not rival Everest in height. The ascent of Fitz Roy gave the green light to this type of expedition climbing. Many of the greatest peaks of the world had been scaled and now climbers would begin to scrutinize the more challenging faces, couloirs, ridges and buttresses. In Terray's autobiography, **Conquistadors of the Useless,** he named Fitz Roy as his hardest climb. "A great ascent is more than the sum of its severe pitches. The remoteness of Fitz Roy from all possibility of help, the almost incessant bad weather, the verglas with which it is plastered, and above all the terrible winds which make climbing on it mortally dangerous, render its ascent more complex, hazardous and exhausting than anything to be found in the Alps."

---

5. West faces of Fitz Roy, Poincenot, Torre Innominata and Saint Exupery from Cerro Torre. The Supercouloir route on Fitz Roy lies just out of view around the left side, the Czech West Face route follows the diagonal gash up the center of Fitz Roy while the America route ascends just left of the right skyline. The Poincenot 1977 route follows the great diagonal ramp on the West Face. *Nikon FM, 20mm lens, K 64*

6. Bobby Knight leading a difficult corner on the second ascent of the North Pillar of Fitz Roy. *Nikon FM, 20mm lens, K 64*

7. Evening on the North Pillar of Fitz Roy. We traversed one rope length across ledges to our second bivouac. *Nikon FM, 20mm lens, K 64*

8. North Pillar of Fitz Roy from the east from Col Superior; this Andean Condor soared by on rising air currents. *Nikon FM, 43-86mm lens, K 64*

The principal factor that sets the monolith apart from other mountains is unpredictability. Storms develop rapidly and with uncanny treachery. Fitz Roy does not match the Himalaya in height, yet it holds a special challenge for climbers.

First ascent of Aguja Poincenot: 1962

With the ascent of Fitz Roy, and the Italian expeditions to Cerro Torre in 1958 and 1959, interest in Patagonian climbing increased rapidly. In the summer of 1961 a group of Irish climbers invited Don Whillans to join them on an expedition to Poincenot. This spire, named for Jacques Poincenot who died on the 1952 French Fitz Roy expedition, is slightly over a kilometer south of Fitz Roy. The 3036 meter tooth of granite is bordered on the east by the Río Blanco Glacier and on the northeast by the Piedras Glacier. For many hundreds of meters, smooth rock walls offer few lines of weakness and the overall symmetry of the mountain is very appealing. Whillans was especially attracted to the spire but found cash to be in short supply. He later wrote of how he solved the dilemma. "I couldn't afford it, and I would have to be stern with myself.... My wife looked up from her knitting and said, 'Why don't you sell the bike?' (his motorcycle) and the problem was solved."

Don Whillans was no novice climber. Since 1950 he had scaled the Bonatti Pillar and Walker Spur in the Alps and had completed a new route on Mont Blanc up the Central Pillar of Frêney in 1961. Whillans and the Irish climbers, Frank Cochrane, Francis Beloe, Clive Burland, George Narramore and Tony Kavanagh, struggled to leave Britain for Patagonia. An airline strike held them up for two weeks; when they finally arrived in Buenos Aires their problems had only begun. Their equipment had been shipped by boat but the longshoremen were reluctant to unearth its location in the vast docks of Buenos Aires. Two weeks trickled away, as did many of the seven hundred cans of *Export Guinness* the expedition had brought with them. Whillans took a break one afternoon, popped open a *Guinness* , and found that by accident he was sitting on a box of their missing gear.

It took three more days to clear the equipment from the barge; five more days passed while the army plane they were to fly on was delayed. Finally, after Christmas, the plane took off but quickly returned to the airport with engine trouble. Stuck 64 kilometers from Poincenot and Fitz Roy, a week of perfect weather slipped by as the frustrated group waited for a truck to transport them across the Río Las Vueltes. Whillans became worried and the *Guinness* continued to dwindle. "Stories of one day's good weather in a season made us think we were wasting seven years' good weather."

The expedition planned to use the 1952 French base camp. An elderly German, Herr Stanhardt, who now occupied Madsen's estancia, led them by horse to the site. In less than a week the team established three camps, the last a snow cave at Col Superior near the Piedras Glacier, just below Poincenot. Whillans and Kavanagh fixed three hundred meters of hemp rope up the diagonal ramp of ice on the east face that leads to the southeast ridge. For three days they climbed primarily on ice tilted at fifty degrees or steeper and anchored the ropes to ensure a safe retreat in a storm. One obstacle remained between the ice ramp and the shoulder below the southeast ridge; an ice filled chimney capped by an overhang. Whillans cut steps in the ice and with the help of a knee jam squirmed past the projection. The pair dumped a load of pitons and food at the base of the ridge and descended the ramp in a snowstorm as windblown snow swept the face. For a week and a half the storm persisted. Snow built up three meters thick around the snow cave until a crack appeared in the roof. They retreated to base camp.

When the weather improved, Whillans found only Frank Cochrane was interested in joining him in a summit attempt. The two left Camp II at 3 am on 31 January and cramponed up the frozen Piedras Glacier under the light of a bright moon. By late morning they had reclimbed the fixed ropes and were standing on the southeast ridge, facing a maturing storm. They believed the summit to be another 240 meters above them and the route appeared reasonable. But dark clouds were boiling up to the west, and a powerful wind had already begun to batter the spire. "I don't like the looks of the weather," said Cochrane.

"We've come a fair way. No point in giving up until it becomes really hopeless," responded Whillans.

All through the afternoon, Whillans led every pitch up the coarse rock, banging in pitons now and then and writhing up chimneys. The wind increased as the snowflakes shot straight up into the air. After three hundred meters of steep climbing up cracks and rough rock they reached the tiny summit. Each took turns straddling the fin of rock for photographs. With the storm in full swing there was no time to dally, so they hammered in a French piton in memory of Jaques Poincenot and started down. Whillans described the descent. "Our descent of the ridge was mainly accomplished by climbing, as it was impossible to throw the abseil rope down because of the wind; it simply refused to drop, waving and thrashing about, sometimes shooting vertically into the air."

Twenty hours after beginning the climb, Whillans and Cochrane returned to their ice cave tired, hungry and thirsty. Up above, Poincenot had disappearred into the black night and thick cloud of the tempest.

Fitz Roy's Supercouloir: 1965

Two decades after the initial ascent of the Supercouloir, Bobby Knight and I arrived in Los Glaciares National Park to attempt the North Pillar of Fitz Roy. Bobby had climbed extensively in Yosemite, had nearly made the summit of Mount Huntington, Alaska in 1980 by a difficult ice route and had climbed with me on a long alpine route in Washington the same year. Our gear and food lay scattered about the grass and we had just brewed up a mug of cocoa when a tall man with gleaming white teeth and attired in *Patagonia* clothing strolled up. "Are you going to climb the Feetz Roy?" he asked in an Argentine accent. "Well, uh, we are going to try," I replied. This man seemed to know something about climbing and the *Patagonia* clothing was mighty suspicious, as he couldn't have acquired it in Argentina. "Are you a climber?" "Yes." "Have you been to Fitz Roy before?" "Eighteen times," he said with a laugh. "What's your name?" "Fonrouge." My eyes lit up and a thrill passed through me like a mild electric current. All I could say was, "Ah, the Supercouloir". It was enough, for his eyes twinkled and a wide smile revealed more perfect teeth. Later he admitted that it was a great feeling for him that I had recognized his name and associated it with the Supercouloir.

I asked Fonrouge why climbers came here to climb and often returned. "You get a feeling here you do not get from Peru or Nepal, because of the strength of the elements. Patagonia contains the ideal mountains; steep, difficult, cold and aesthetic."

Since 1965 the Supercouloir has been the scene of countless attempts, yet seldom have climbers reached the summit by this route. The elegant line it forms and the possibility of gaining the top quickly by climbing mainly on snow and ice has lured top alpinists from around the world. Though attractive, the couloir is a very deceptive route. Between the walls of the gully the climber is protected from the wind, but near its top he must exit to a gendarmed ridge and become exposed to the full force of any storm in progress. This is a crucial spot on the climb, one that has defeated many parties. The giant gash is the most dangerous route on Fitz Roy to descend in a storm. It is a collection funnel for falling rocks, ice and snow, which accumulate into avalanches that sweep climbers off their feet.

It is also the only place I know of where a wind tornado has been observed during a climb. In 1981, Gino Buscaini photographed the two meter wide atmospheric phenomenon while ascending the Supercouloir with his wife Silvia Metzeltin. The lethal, silvery snake hovered in the uppermost part of the couloir on a clear day without another cloud in the sky. Despite the dangers, climbers go back year after year in hopes of getting good conditions in the couloir and a few days of windless weather. The German climber Reinhard

Karl talked of why he returned to try the Supercouloir. "I knew that here the exception to the rule was rare, that climbing was not self assertion, but battle, a boxing match where you're knocked out by wind, weather, and your taut hopes until you crawl from the ring on all fours when you've been beaten. I knew all this and still I'd returned."

The fifteen hundred meter high couloir that cleaves the northwest side of Fitz Roy almost in two, had been attempted by Argentine climbers in 1962 and in 1965, a month before Fonrouge and Carlos Comesaña arrived. This latter attempt was organized by Otto Weisskopf and Carlos Botazzi but, owing to their lack of conditioning, they climbed less than halfway up the route after spending three days on the mountain. Fonrouge and Comesaña arrived at Fitz Roy in early January with Antonio Misson, Martin Donovan and Jorge Ruiz Luque in support. More than one present day climber has scratched his head and wondered how Fonrouge (then aged twenty) and Comesaña made the first ascent, when so many skilled parties in the 1970s and 1980s have failed.

At the age of fifteen, Fonrouge completed the second ascent of the North Tower of Paine in Chilean Patagonia with his Argentine companions. At seventeen, he attempted the 1650 meter West Face of Fitz Roy alpine style with one partner. They didn't get very high, but the attempt alone was way ahead of its time. The Alps and the mountains of Antarctica further honed his skills for the Supercouloir. He wanted to climb Fitz Roy more than anything else in the world. Motivation is often the underlying factor that tips the scales toward success in the mountains and Fonrouge certainly posessed it.

Following a warmup climb and first ascent of nearby Guillaumet, Fonrouge and Comesaña hiked the sixteen kilometers from a base camp in the Rio Eléctrico Valley to the start of the Supercouloir on 14 January. They bivouaced by hanging hammocks inside the bergschrund and tried to sleep. The weather was perfect. In the morning the two excited climbers stowed bivy gear, food and wooden wedges for the climb in their sacks and organized their 73 meter rope, sixteen pitons and ice screws for the ascent.

On the first day Fonrouge and Comesaña ascended frozen snow, an ideal climbing condition, initially at an angle of fifty degrees. Crampons and axe picks bit solidly into ice as the couloir steepened. Only the whirring sound of falling rocks disturbed the quiet walls. Where the couloir split into two branches, the climbers left behind one pair of crampons, ice axes and overboots and began working their way up difficult rock. Chimneys and overhangs slowed their progress and made route finding difficult. Placing a piton for direct aid and a traverse consumed the remaining light.

The weary pair hung hammocks from the wall and heated water for hot drinks. They had climbed nine hundred meters but over six hundred meters still separated them from the summit. Above lay the unknown.

In the morning Fonrouge and Comesaña wriggled out of their hammocks. Aching muscles responded slowly as they resumed the battle up over icy slabs and overhanging rock to the top of the couloir. A gendarmed ridge was the final obstacle separating them from the summit. For several hours Fonrouge and Comesaña threaded their way around and over ice plastered towers of rock.

The sun was still bright whan they stopped at 7 pm for peanuts and candies, with the summit snowfield in sight. In another hour the jubilant pair stood at the very top of Fitz Roy, where they replaced Terray's carabiner with an Argentine flag. Tears filled their eyes as they hugged. This summit was their dream of a lifetime. For the rest of their lives they might never again feel the satisfaction the Supercouloir provided. Fonrouge recalled, "I felt a state of grace, of ultimate calm; the end of a dream!"

Their descent of the Supercouloir was a nightmare. The storm arrived with wind and snow after their third bivouac; the pair sacrificed pitons, ice screws, slings and hammer cords for rappel anchors. Their rope became stiff from the cold, and difficult to retrieve. Finally, four pitches above the bottom the wind tangled the rope and it became hopelessly stuck. They cut off what remained and descended separately to the bottom. For four days the Supercouloir had embraced the two alpinists, then released them unharmed. In the years following, other climbers were not as fortunate; more than one lost his life in the gigantic gully.

Southwest Ridge of Fitz Roy: 1968

Two years after the ascent of the Supercouloir, Fonrouge paid a visit to the United States and, while climbing in California, met Yvon Chouinard and Doug Tompkins. Chouinard, with various partners, had pioneered many big wall climbs in Yosemite Valley and put up a number of first ascents on ice and mixed routes in the Canadian Rockies. He was also a designer and manufacturer of climbing hardware in California. Tompkins had begun rock climbing at the age of twelve in the Shawangunks, was climbing mountains in the Tetons and Wind Rivers by the age of fifteen and making ascents of big mountains in the Alps and Andes by his late teens. Fascinated by the granite colossus they had seen in Fonrouge's slides, Chouinard and Tompkins quickly contacted another climber, the ex-patriate Briton Chris Jones, ski racer Dick Dorworth and cinematographer Lito Tejada-Flores to round out the group.

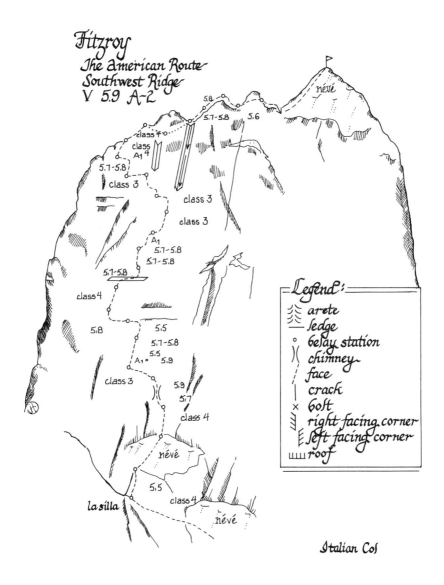

Fitzroy
The American Route
Southwest Ridge
V 5.9 A-2

5.8
5.7-5.8
5.6
néve
class 4
class
A1 4
5.7-5.8
class 3
class 3
class 3
A1
5.7-5.8
5.7-5.8
5.1-5.8
class 4
5.8
5.5
5.7-5.8
5.5
A1
5.9
class 3
5.9
5.7
class 4

Legend:
arete
ledge
belay station
chimney
face
crack
× bolt
right facing corner
left facing corner
roof

néve
5.5
la silla
class 4
néve

Italian Col

Most expeditions are content to pick one goal; to reach the summit. Not so the ambitious *Funhogs*, as they called themselves. The five adventurers wanted to return home with a 16mm color movie as well. I saw the film in college four years after their ascent and was impressed by the size of Fitz Roy and the long powerful storms the expedition endured. I had a strong desire to give up my books and take off on a voyage such as theirs.

For five months the Californians travelled through South America surfing, skiing on snow and sand, climbing volcanoes and eating. At one point in Guatemala, machine gun toting soldiers rousted the *Funhogs* out of their sleeping bags at night to check their passports. In Bariloche the group spent a month climbing on the granite spires of Catedrál to prepare for Fitz Roy. Before leaving Bariloche, the climbers purchased all the remaining needed food; then set out on the final sixteen hundred kilometer leg of the journey. After 26,500 kilometers of driving they saw their objective. Even at a distance of ninety kilometers Fitz Roy dominated the horizon. It is not a mountain nestled among other peaks; it stands alone, leaving every alpinist that has laid eyes on it stunned. For the Americans, the surfing and skiing had come to an end.

In the first eight days of good weather the group carried their gear and two weeks' food up to the couloir below the Italian Col on Fitz Roy's south side. The weather turned bad; the climbers scurried back down to base camp in the beech forest. Then it turned good and they hurried back up to the couloir and climbed to the Italian Col. Here they dug a snow cave just west of the start of the French route and investigated a possible unclimbed line up the Southwest Ridge. They anticipated getting started immediately on the route but the weather dictated a different scenario. Tompkins was frustrated. "Finally we got up and established in a day or two and got in this monstrous goddam storm that lasted twenty-five days." For fifteen of them, very little happened beyond the walls of the cave. Tompkins told me later, "We got into sleeping, dozing and into kinda daydreaming, kinda almost a semi-hypnotic state and then we'd tell about dreams and tell stories. I had been reading some things about Freud's studies of dreams, so I already knew some techniques about how to remember dreams and how to relate dreams to other things."

With their food gone, they retreated to base camp. Tejada-Flores and Tompkins drove 160 kilometers to the nearest town and bought more. The pair returned to base camp with sixty-eight kilos of food and hopes of gaining the summit. After another false start and a six day storm, the climbers returned to their cave with food for three weeks, determined to finish the climb. During the night the skies cleared and at 2:30 the next morning they began traversing snow and ice to the base of the rock. Without telling the others,

Tompkins had set the alarm clock an hour earlier the night before to speed up the morning ritual of dressing and eating breakfast.

Tompkins and Chouinard had been climbing partners before the trip and did the leading; Tejada-Flores jumared and filmed the climbing; Dorworth followed next; and Jones cleaned the ropes. Throughout the climb everyone took extra precautions with Dorworth, such as making sure he was safely clipped into anchors at belay stations. Although a good athlete, he lacked the experience of the other four. According to Tompkins, "Somebody would have to watch him all the time." Despite the size of the party, the Californians climbed faster on the first ascent than many subsequent small expeditions that failed to make the summit. They left bivouac bags and extra clothing behind, these were soaking wet from the many humid days spent in the snow cave. Chouinard felt that carrying less helped their speed on the climb. "We climbed for twenty-three straight hours to the summit and back; it was a race with both the weather and our deteriorating equipment. Not having the bivouac gear forced us to move quickly and continuously."

They spent all day ascending crack systems and corners, relying on some aid and a lot of free climbing. Ice filled the cracks, higher up the rock was caked in rime. Where the rock remained bare, extremely solid nubbins and crystals provided superb face climbing. At 2 pm they reached a notch directly above the Supercouloir. Clouds from the ice cap streamed upwards out of the big gully. (Four years later the British climbers Dave Nicol, Ian Wade, Mo Anthoine and Eddie Birch completed a new route up the South Buttress of Fitz Roy. Their line finished above the Supercouloir near the Southwest Ridge, where Nicol gaped at the chasm below. "Translucent dinner plates of ice floated up from the depths like ghostly familiars or eldritch spirits.")

As the air pressure dropped the Americans grew anxious. Their progress was hampered by a ridge of snowy gendarmes that guarded access to the summit slopes. For four hours the group clambered around and over the towers of rock as the wind began to blow fiercely. On the gentle boulder studded snowslopes they plodded upwards, as the wind carried their ropes in airborne arcs away from them. At 7 pm the group became the third party to stand on Fitz Roy's highest point.

The formidable mountain had certainly attracted skilled alpinists from around the world. De Agostini's book inspired Terray and the French climbers to climb Fitz Roy. Terray and Magnone had in turn spurred Fonrouge and Comesaña. Fonrouge's visit to the United States further stimulated the Americans to try Fitz Roy. With the knowledge gained from their predecessors, the Americans had completed yet another page in the growing volume of Patagonian climbing history.

Without hesitation, the five climbers started their descent into swirling clouds and high wind. At 2 am it was too dark to continue rappelling; the tired men bivouaced. After a cold night, they continued on down until, six pitches above their cave, a rope, whipped by the intense wind, caught on a flake. They cut the rope and, using a spare line to rappel, regained their cave at 11 am. Fifteen years later three climbers on the Southwest Ridge also bivouaced during the descent but in a greater storm. Americans Scott Backes and Scott Cole and Frenchman Yves Asiter spent the night near the same place as the Chouinard party in 1968. A gust of wind uprooted Backes from the ledge, spun him around, and deposited him on the other side of his companions.

The American Route has become the most popular line on Fitz Roy for modern parties. The climbing is not exceedingly difficult (see Appendix III), there are only several pitches of aid and the route can be climbed from Col Superior and back with one bivouac. But the mountain is still Fitz Roy, on which even the easiest route demands respect.

West Face of Aguja Poincenot: 1977

Speed is essential in Patagonia. Because the mountains are low in height relative to other ranges, a climber need not worry about contracting pulmonary or cerebral edema from gaining elevation too quickly. Climbs that can be accomplished quickly make better use of short spells of good weather; climbers are exposed to objective hazards for a briefer time. Objective hazards are those over which the climber has no control; storms, rockfall, icefall and lightning. The nature of a route dictates whether the mountain can be climbed quickly or not. Faces that are less than vertical offer more free climbing potential; climbers can move more quickly when not using direct aid.

One route that lends itself to a rapid ascent is the twelve hundred meter high West Face of Poincenot. The mountain's west wall is slashed diagonally by two giant ramps that sweep upwards to intersect the southwest buttress and the broken slopes below the summit. In 1977 both ramps were unclimbed; the longer one looked the easier. Two British climbers, Alan Rouse and Rab Carrington, in top shape from over a month of climbing in the Fitz Roy region, felt they could climb Poincenot in a day if they travelled light. From a bivouac site below the face, they packed four small chocolate bars, lightweight sleeping bags, a bivy sac, headlamps, ten nuts and six pitons.

Before dawn the pair soloed up an ice gully to gain the long ramp of rock. Rouse described the ascent of the couloir. "We climbed quickly at night, and seldom spoke as we soloed in this ominous place. The remains of a human body poked out of a wide crack." The body was probably that of Argentine Hugo Bela, who was killed in an accident just below the Silla in 1971.

Once out of the gully, Rouse and Carrington climbed quickly up verglas coated rock; then front pointed up narrow runnels of ice. Carrington enjoyed the climbing and later wrote, "...with light sacks, the climbing was magic; a touch of mixed climbing here, an iced up groove there, then on tiptoe up the flaky slabs, getting higher and higher." In the upper portion of the ramp they resorted to face climbing and layback moves as the rock became drier. The final three hundred meters of excellent rock was split by a multitude of cracks and chimneys. Coarse granite offered good holds for hands and feet. The pair gained the tiny summit two hours before dark, completing the third ascent of the spire and by a new route. From twilight until after dark, they rappelled part way down the wall, spending the night on a ledge. They had run out of water but found puddles beneath a layer of ice, in round, wind eroded holes in the rock. Twenty more rappels remained to the bottom but they had their summit and slept warm. Their rapid ascent had paid off, for the climbers reached the bottom just as a storm began to develop.

North Pillar of Fitz Roy: 1979

Italians Renato Casarotto, his wife Goretta, Giovanni Maiori and Luigi Zen reached Fitz Roy on 20 November 1978. During the following sixteen days the three men carried loads up to Col Superior and established an advance camp for an assault on the unclimbed North Pillar. During this period, "normal" meteorological conditions prevailed; snow, rime, rain, clouds and, of course, wind. The fifteen hundred meter high column of rock was an apalling sight. On some days it would appear frosty white from snow and rime; on others the bare walls glistened with water from melting snow. The pillar rose in a steep smooth line towards the summit; climbing it would be no picnic.

With the expedition barely under way, Maiori and Zen became disgusted with the bad weather and, on 6 December, they returned to Italy. Renato and Goretta Casarotto remained behind, bound to Fitz Roy by an invisible force. Renato decided to solo the mountain. He was not new to soloing, having completed the first solo winter ascents of the Simon-Rossi route on the North Face of Monte Pelmo in 1974 and the Andrich-Fae route on the Punta Civetta the following year; both routes in the Dolomites. In 1977 Casarotto spent seventeen days on the North Face of Huascarán in the Cordillera

Blanca, Peru; completing a new route on his own. Casarotto went to work on Fitz Roy, confident he could climb the mountain alone. His wife helped carry loads to the base of the mountain so that he could fix ropes up most of the route. The one-and-a-half kilometer high shaft of granite had never been climbed on; every move the Italian made would be alone and on unknown terrain. Casarotto's own words reveal, in part, what motivated him. "As my experience grew and my activity output intensified, I found myself engaged in a quest for new objectives. This caused me to formulate a series of questions in my mind, to which I had to find the answer. What was the goal toward which I was striving? Basically it was a quest for adventure and for certain values which modern life, with its habit forming daily routine, has practically caused to disappear."

Hideous weather ruled the skies for twenty-five days. A tent which Casarotto had pitched at Col Superior was demolished; he and Goretta relocated themselves in a log hut next to the Rio Blanco nine hundred meters below. The wall below the North Pillar faced east, in the lee of the driving westerly winds. This permitted Casarotto to climb up a 330 meter mixed gully of snow, ice and rock and to fix ropes to the notch between Val de Biois and the start of the pillar.

On 31 December he camped in the notch; the next day he began to work up the sheer face of the pillar. Because of Casarotto's self belay system of prusik knots attached to a rope, he had to lead the pitch placing protection, rappel the pitch and climb up it a second time to clean the anchors. The process was safe, but tedious. He gained 150 meters up strenuous cracks and chimneys and another 150 on 2 January. The wind increased on the third day and permitted him to progress only two-and-a-half pitches of progress. It diminished on the fourth as Casarotto inched his way up cracks and steps on the east corner of the pillar. Fixing his last rope on the top of the pillar, he descended quickly to the relative security of the battered bivouac tent in the notch.

Another storm pinned the Italian inside his tent for a day. On 6 January he reascended the ropes with the intention of climbing all the way to Fitz Roy's summit. But getting off the pillar and into the notch below the north face required three difficult pendulums. To further hamper the lone climber's progress, a wet cold wind deposited a coating of verglas over the rock. Retreat was mandatory, rappelling the glazed ropes demanded extreme caution. He continued on down to base camp and waited for eight days while the wind chewed relentlessly on his precious ropes anchored to the mountain.

Casarotto returned to the lower notch on the 17th, stayed overnight, and started for the summit again the following morning. The wind had damaged his rope; requiring repairs as he climbed late into the night. Between the North Pillar and North Face of Fitz Roy is a small ridge of gendarmes and loose blocks that forms the bottom of the upper notch. In this eerie place of sporadic rock and icefall, Casarotto passed a tentless night.

In the morning the rock was covered in snow and ice but the wind held back. Casarotto jammed up difficult cracks, resorted to aid in places and, 180 meters above the upper notch, gained the lower angled slopes below the top. Late in the afternoon on 19 January he stood elated on the jumbled boulders of the summit. Several years later he reflected on his solo ascents. "I knew that I was on the right road and that solo climbing would ultimately provide my personal fulfillment. As I analysed my actions, I realised that I was not interested in the pursuit of difficulty for difficulty's sake. My chosen routes had to have real, positive attraction. The factors which motivate me to climb are a need for action, a desire for the unknown and a longing for mental and physical commitment; which may be total."

Casarotto could not have chosen a finer and more demanding objective than the North Pillar of Fitz Roy and his impressive feat of climbing endurance will rank among the most significant ascents achieved worldwide.

West Face of Fitz Roy: 1983

The massive and complex West Face of Fitz Roy rises 2400 meters above the head of the Torre Glacier. Even though the first seven hundred meters are low angle and not too difficult, they must still be climbed and are subjected to serious rockfall. José Luis Fonrouge and a companion made the first attempt on the face in 1962 without any fixed ropes. In 1977 Alan Rouse and Rab Carrington climbed eighteen hundred meters up the wall on their second alpine attempt before the bad weather moved in. Rouse felt the route would go above their high point. "We estimated this final section (six hundred meters) would need two more days. That meant we would need four or five days of continuous good weather. This seemed to us a remote possibility."

Perhaps it was these very words written by Rouse that prompted a Czech expedition to mount a siege on the steep portion of the West Face early in 1982. Daniel Bakos, Zdenek Brabec, Robert Gálfy, Dusan Kovac, Michal Orolin and Vladimir Petrik spent two months working on the route. From a base camp near Lago Torre they reached the upper part of the face on their fourth attempt. On their first try the Czechs ascended the first seven hundred meters above the Torre Glacier in a single day with heavy packs, not being hampered by the oxygen starved air typical of Himalayan peaks.

But difficult climbing higher up and atrocious weather finally killed their hopes. Robert Gálfy knew they were finished at their last bivouac. "In the evening we saw heavy clouds over Cerro Torre. The wind did not calm down all night. Snow started to fall. In the morning strong winds and new snow forced us to descend."

Nine months later the Czechs came back to try Fitz Roy again. Of the six original climbers, Brabec, Gálfy, Orolin and Petrik returned, while Milan Hoholik, Dr. Frantisek Kele and Tibor Surka joined the expedition. From the previous trip the Czechs had learned that it would be wiser to climb the West Face from the Fitz Roy Glacier and the Piedra Fraile base camp, thus eliminating the dangerous seven hundred meter start above the Torre Glacier and shortening the route.

Between 5 and 15 December the group carried loads to the base of the Supercouloir (near the west Face) and dug a snow cave. From their cave, in forty minutes the climbers could reach a ridge that led to the West Face to meet up with the 1982 route. On the 17th the climbers ascended slabs in the rain to find their ropes from the earlier 1982 attempt damaged by wind and rockfall. Five days later they climbed up the route again to a point 150 meters below the original high point where bad weather had forced a retreat.

On 28 December the skies finally cleared again and Brabec, Gálfy, Orolin and Petrik ascended the fixed ropes to the former high point. Gálfy donned rock shoes and led an overhanging chimney; then another pitch before rappelling to a hammock bivouac. Orolin and Petrik joined Gálfy and Brabec in the evening; the four slept well under the stars. Dawn brought wind, by 7 am it was snowing; nevertheless, Gálfy managed to climb another pitch and fix a rope. He belayed Orolin as powder snow began to slough down the cracks and corners; a sure sign of heavy and ominous weather. Suddenly the rope came tight in Gálfy's hands as his partner fell and pulled a piton. The pair felt it was time to descend and fixed a second rope.

Several days of continuous storm inhibited activity until 2 January 1983. After a false start and a return to the cave, the wind abated and the clouds disappeared. Brabec, Gálfy, Orolin and Petrik jumared back up to their hammock bivouac. The next morning Gálfy and Petrik gained their previous high point in one hour. Petrik led and fixed two ropes from beyond the point where Orolin had fallen, then he and Gálfy traversed right and climbed up to join the southwest ridge route 315 meters below the summit.

The four Czechs continued climbing for four more hours, fixed three ropes, then rappelled back down to good bivouac ledges. During the night the wind returned, the morning was frosty and cold. Metal carabiners and cold granite extracted the last bit of warmth from fingers and hands. Gálfy later commented on the strength of the wind. "As Vlado removes pitons, the increasing wind catches one and wafts it fifteen feet up the crag." Minutes after this incident, Gálfy and Petrik's rope dislodged a stone that bounced off a snow shelf and struck Brabec on the leg, leaving an acrid smell of pulverized rock in the air. The injury was serious; the climbers abandoned the ascent and helped Brabec to rappel and climb down the 2600 meters to the cave.

With Brabec injured, only Gálfy, Orolin and Petrik were able to climb and barely two weeks remained before the expedition had to leave Argentina. At that point success seemed remote. But on 14 January the howling gales subsided and the trio went back up the fixed ropes. They climbed until 7 pm, when they reached the Southwest Ridge; then continued for four more hours up icy rock to a bivouac. Perched just below the final ridge, Gálfy was anxious about going for the summit. "I dare not think about it. Bad weather has driven us off the face eight times! Every few minutes I stare out at the sky from my sleeping bag to see whether it is clear or not."

Following a breakfast of tea and sardines, Orolin took the lead and tackled an unprotected off width crack and chimney with the help of a shoulder stand from Petrik. For several hours the Czechs climbed over and around towers encrusted with ice from ten centimeters to one meter thick. At one spot Orolin stood on an old wooden wedge and in another place grabbed a sling. Speed was everthing. From the last gendarme the alpinists rappelled into a saddle where they left behind surplus hardware before climbing to the summit with axes and crampons.

At 3 pm Gálfy, Orolin and Petrik stood on top of Fitz Roy after completing fifty-seven pitches of climbing on the route. There was no wind, no snow and no rain. Orolin felt very happy. "I sat down and tried to taste this moment, one of the greatest feelings in my life." The expedition had achieved its goal of climbing the improbable West Face. The large amount of fixed rope used on their ascent was removed on the way down.

Although Fitz Roy is not protected by the thin air of its Himalayan, Alaskan or high Andean counterparts, the mountain's defenses are formidable. This relatively small peak was climbed only thirteen times, by eight different routes, between 1952 and 1983. A mountain without any weaknesses is intriguing; the uncertainty of reaching the top, due to the sudden violent storms, makes success all the more rewarding. It is these elements that will lure climbers to Patagonia for years to come.

3

FITZ ROY'S NORTH PILLAR - 1984

Over the past sixteen years I have completed long climbs throughout the North Cascades, Canada, and Alaska. On every expedition my companions and I climbed quickly, without a great deal of equipment. I wanted to use the same approach on the North Pillar of Fitz Roy; no party had climbed it in a lightweight manner and the Pillar had not yet received a second ascent. A few such alpine style climbs had been achieved in Patagonia between 1965 and 1983 but most teams still relied on large groups of climbers, established camps, and lots of gear.

In 1982 Bobby Knight and I had succeeded in climbing the difficult Central Tower of Paine with only 45 meters of fixed rope, no established camps, and no support from other climbers. Our impact on the mountain was minimal, apart from rappel anchors we carried everything off. Reaching the top had reinforced my theory. Lightweight was clearly the way to go, why not try it again on Fitz Roy?

We perceived two major differences between the mountains, however; shape and size. Fitz Roy's giant cone of granite appears as though the summit has been lopped off with a knife, leaving the south side lower than the north. Every face has an impenetrable look that hints at difficult climbing. Fitz Roy offered 45 pitches of fifth class climbing on the North Pillar, compared to 17 pitches on our 1982 climb of the Central Tower of Paine. I had discovered that to climb quickly in Patagonia on a route of such size required tremendous enthusiasm, a willing partner and a lot of luck with the weather.

When Bobby and I first arrived by car in the National Park, we couldn't see Fitz Roy. High winds raked the mountain, bank after bank of clouds engulfed the huge rock walls. For a week we carried twenty to thirty kilo loads to base camp at 762 meters, ten kilometers from the road head. In two more weeks we moved equipment up to Col Superior at 1676 meters and dug a snow cave. From our cave to the base of the wall, across the Piedras Glacier, was a two to three hour walk, depending on the snow conditions. Late in the third week we climbed four pitches up the route and anchored three ropes.

After four and a half weeks in the park with unsettled weather,

Bobby frequently questioned the value of climbing Fitz Roy and I struggled to maintain my drive. Our first foray on the mountain failed halfway up the pillar when our stove failed and a brief snowstorm plastered the face. We climbed slightly more than halfway up the North Pillar a second time only to face another storm during the night and indecision in the morning. I awoke before Bobby and thought about our position. If we continued up, our commitment would increase with every pitch.

A layer of fresh snow had dusted my bivy sac during the night. The sight of those millions of tiny snow crystals made me feel even colder now that morning had arrived. Even in the summertime, at 49 degrees south latitude, the nights seemed long. Afraid to look at the sky and confront bad news, I kept staring at the wrinkled and faded yellow *Gore-Tex* covering my legs and feet. Shifting my position a little created micro avalanches of snow on the steep sides of the sac. Small slabs a centimeter thick poured down on the gravel covered ledge. I raised my head a few degrees to direct my vision eastwards. A warm light streamed down between layers of dark clouds and illuminated a winding river far below. I wondered if the sun would ever reach the ledge and melt the snow.

My toes remained numb with cold and every joint in my body felt stiff. A few pea sized granite pebbles had left an impression on my bottom and, as a result, it was sore on the right side. I craved additional sleep but at this point only movement would bring back the feeling in my extremities. Bobby and I would have been more comfy had we not left our sleeping bags and pads thirteen pitches below, at the first bivy. We were cold but that extra five kilos could have slowed our ascent considerably. When the time arrived to get moving, Bobby was still dozing. He needed to. The previous day, our second on the route, we had exhausted ourselves trying to find the way.

Just before dark that night, the route had diverged with two cracks disappearing into the fog. The left hand fissure oozed water and looked too steep to climb free. The right crack was dry and not as steep. I had stemmed wide with one foot in a corner and the other in the crack until my legs would stretch no more. Inching up, my fingers wormed into a thin crack as my eyes searched for small crystals to place my feet on. After forty meters of climbing, my forearms began to burn with fatigue, and the crack I was following was leading towards blank rock. I attempted a half dozen pendulums into the left hand crack but without success. Bobby thought we should rappel 45 meters back down to a good ledge. I had wasted more than an hour and could only agree with his suggestion.

Around midnight a moisture laden storm came pouring out of the inky sky. Hail, snow and water flowed down the cracks and gushed out directly at Bobby. He danced about trying to avoid the torrent and to divert the water by rearranging rocks and digging tiny ditches. During his moment of frustration I saw an opportunity and handed over my water bottle for a refill. Thirst nagged at my throat but the gesture irritated Bobby and did nothing to ease his discomfort.

Our minature stove hissed at me as I screwed in a fresh butane cartridge. The thought of a hot drink would at least warm my spirits, if not my feet; but the stove's dull roar lulled me back to sleep. I awoke to find the water boiling with the pot less than half filled. I finally brewed up some hot *Tang* and cocoa, knowing Bobby could not resist the smell of steaming Argentine *Nesquick*. I sipped the hot sweet liquid as I worried about the difficulty of the climbing above. This was, after all, the 1500 meter tall North Pillar of Fitz Roy; neither Bobby nor I could guess just how big or how difficult it might be. How many more nights we would spend on this colossal mountain would depend on the amount of aid needed and, totally beyond our control, the fickle weather.

So far the weather had been unbelievably good. For ten days straight the wind had blown very little, while clouds filled the valleys and covered the Patagonian Ice Cap. Now, from our perch at 2590 meters and upwards, the sky remained blue and we could catch glimpses of it from inside Fitz Roy's private cloud that cloaked the upper half of the granite monolith. We realized it could not last and that somewhere between the Pacific Ocean and the mountain must lurk a massive amount of moist air waiting for the right moment to strike. In Patagonia, every day of good weather makes a climber feel as though he is living on borrowed time. Alpinists can never shake off the feeling that only moments away the mother of storms is brewing winds that will pluck the fixed pitons right out of the wall. Other climbers had found rappelling and retrieving ropes during these storms desperately hard.

The Swiss climber Thomas Wüschner knew a lot about Patagonian storms. Aside from his extensive experience in the Alps, he had climbed Fitz Roy, Cerro Torre, and Poincenot. He had lingered in the beech forest after his recent climb of Poincenot, waiting to try another peak. "In storm you must leave carabiner on abseil anchors", commented Thomas before we began our climb. "Why's that?", I asked. "The rope freeze and you cannot pull rope down." The statement formed a crisp image in my mind as we sat on our ledge 760 meters above the Piedras Glacier, yet only halfway to the summit. Now, high on the pillar, I studied Bobby's tired face as he slept. Deep creases existed where none were before. The wind, sun, and anxiety had done their work on him.

When Bobby agreed to go with me to Fitz Roy, he was uncertain as to the amount of energy he would have for the North Pillar and pointed out I might have to take up the slack at times. I was so overjoyed at having a partner that I agreed to anything Bobby said. Later, on the climb, when he expressed doubts about the route or weather, I continued to supply the optimism. Frequently I would say, "Let's just go a pitch higher and have a look." Perhaps it was only his way of letting out his feelings and releasing tension. Our level of motivation was different and dealing with that was hard on us but I realize now there are very few people with whom I am as compatible with as with Bobby. We always manage to talk problems out, arrive at a decision and remain friends after our trips are over.

Throughout the expedition we had worked our way through the many hassles of foreign travel. We each had a personal style of accomplishing tasks and, at times, that created friction. As we approached the point where the climbing began I could see that major differences existed as to our expectations and goals. I talked about reaching the summit of Fitz Roy while Bobby said he would be satisfied to reach the top of the North Pillar, twelve hundred meters below the summit. I wondered if this morning would find us arguing or just exchanging small talk over breakfast.

With the snowstorm on the second night, I thought the game was over but the sun came out and tendrils of vapor swirled upwards as the wet rock began to dry out. Even if the weather remained good during the day, success was not assured. Bobby's hands had started to crack and bleed and my stomach was aching from the nervous tension of the climb. "Cocoa's ready," I signaled to Bobby. Very little can upset Bobby when he is tucking away his hot chocolate and after the cup was drained I detected a slight sparkle in those weary eyes. We might reach the top after all.

The slimy crack I had avoided the night before now appeared our only option. I climbed on direct aid for the first 24 meters, alternating placements with one #3+ and one #4 Friend. I began wedging my hands and free climbing as the crack dried out and narrowed in size. We left the stove and bivy sacs on the ledge at our second bivouac, in hopes of trimming down our gear a bit so that we could move faster but the ease of carrying a lighter pack hardly kept pace with our continual loss of energy. All we had for food was a small hunk of cheese and some dried pears.

Water, however, was not in short supply. Above me a squeeze chimney and off width crack dripped with the stuff. Bobby led the chimney pitch methodically and ran out of rope just as the big crack began to narrow. That meant I would have to lead the fifteen to eighteen centimeter fissure which glistened with water and flared slightly. Usually, I have a ravenous appetite for cracks of that size but this one lacked appeal. Luckily, a thin crack alongside accepted pitons and small stoppers nicely and allowed me to circumvent the nasty rent in the wall. The second crack eventually merged with the first and I was forced to step out of aid stirrups and free climb the upper part of the wide crack. A good deal of writhing and heavy breathing finally put the damp obstacle below us. Our progress was meager. We had been climbing all day and only completed five pitches.

That didn't seem so bad when I thought about Renato Casarotto spending forty-three days on the first ascent of the North Pillar in 1979. Casarotto exhibited his determination on Fitz Roy by slowly pushing his route higher whenever the weather allowed. He climbed just sixty meters during a stormy day in late December and 106 meters on another day. But he kept at it and finished the elegant route. We found Casarotto's fixed pitons and scraps of rope here and there, although our line deviated from his on many pitches. The faded and tattered equipment fascinated me. I had read descriptions of the gear abandoned on Cerro Torre by climbers performing hasty retreats. Racks of hardware, coiled ropes, pitons, carabiners and fixed ropes festooned that frosty spire. But with Casarotto it was different. He climbed the North Pillar, anchored ropes, made the summit, retreated and then left behind perfectly good equipment instead of carrying it down. The ropes were probably in bad shape and not cut loose because he rappelled them instead of setting up retrievable ropes for each rappel. But why did he leave everything else? At his bivouac 335 meters above the glacier we found a demolished tent, two rucksacks (one full of rusted cans of food), two functional butane stoves, a rock hammer, slings and a whole rack of carabiners and pitons, a couple of which were titanium. Perhaps he had plenty of money and didn't need the gear, since much of his equipment was donated by manufacturers. Or maybe, after six weeks soloing the pillar, he was so anxious to get off the mountain that little else mattered.

Casarotto's motives puzzled me and I wanted to whip out my knife and at least cut free the sun bleached fixed ropes but another part of me marvelled at those traces of human passage. Six years ago this man had climbed every pitch on the mountain by himself, hauled and fixed over one and a half kilometers of rope and carried up sackfuls of pitons, carabiners, and wooden wedges. His task demanded respect; I felt it best not to disturb the vertical museum too much.

Climbing past the old ropes and wedges had taken most of the day and it was getting late. I removed the plastic outer boots from my rock shoes and led up thin cracks and over solid golf ball sized knobs of granite. Snow mushrooms two to three meters high marked the top of the North Pillar but the notch between the pillar and the main wall of Fitz Roy was enveloped in fog. The place had a dank smell and it was obvious we could climb no further in the dark.

I chopped the ice from a 1 x 1½ meter sized ledge as Bobby kicked off unwanted rocks. Our headlamps sent sporadic rays of light into the gloom as our proposed bed improved. It began to snow as we sat down on the ropes with nothing for warmth but our clothing. After sharing the last scrap of cheese the night grew colder and any further discussion between us evaporated. Our thoughts followed separate channels and hunger knawed at our stomachs. I remembered another of Wuschner's responses when I asked him if he exercised to stay in shape during the long storms in Patagonia. "No. If you here a month you don't eat much at first, then you eat more. You start in the morning and eat all day. It is the only work here." At the time he was systematically consuming boxes of cookies dunked in coffee heavily laden with milk and sugar. The man's thighs were as big as my waist and it looked as though he needed a lot of food to fill them up. If only I had followed the example Wüschner set, I might have had a few more pounds of fat to burn through the night.

The fog ebbed, revealing stars above, and the faint voices of other people drifted toward us. Three weeks earlier we had met five Polish climbers who had planned to siege a new route up the pillar's west side. They must have reached the notch, although in the dark it was difficult to be sure. Communicating with them would have served no purpose as we could not reach them. The Poles probably had sleeping bags and hot food at their bivouac but not us. Siege climbing did have its advantages. I ached for morning to arrive and with it the possibility of sunshine and warmth.

Around 5 am the sun did hit us. My hunger was worse. This was our fourth day on the mountain and it was clear. Although I felt giddy, my desire to finish the climb had not yet died. Bobby and I cut steps across steep snow to the pillar's top and then did two rappels down into the notch. Remembering how cold and hungry we were the night before made the sight of the Polish camp in the notch even more shocking.

On boulders and level spaces they had spread out their equipment. They had every form of comfort. Yellow bivy sacs, blue bivy sacs, aluminized space blankets, blue foam pads, down sleeping bags, various pots, two butane stoves, plastic bags of cereal, dried fruit, margarine and sugar littered the granite slabs. I caught a whiff of hot cereal cooking and greeted the Poles as they crawled from sleeping bags and fitted cold stiff boots on their feet. Food was on my mind and I knew good film was difficult to come by in Poland, so I traded the expedition photographer (Michal Kochanczak) a roll of *Ektachrome* film for a pot of instant cornmeal. He apologized for the flecks of windblown gravel that peppered the food but our starved bodies accepted both vegetable and mineral greedily. I managed a great smile. The day was 24 December and the weather was calm.

Bobby led up cracks and flakes to a point where the wall poured with snowmelt. He winced at the prospect of getting soaked and admitted that he had no desire to go to the summit. Bobby had made the top of the pillar, that was the goal he had set for himself. I had set the summit of Fitz Roy as my goal, a good three hundred meters higher. Inside my head a pounding exasperation began to mount. The day was damned perfect and here we sat arguing when we could be climbing. Thirty minutes later Bobby agreed to go to the summit if we could jumar the ropes the Poles had fixed the day before. Michal had said to us that morning, "We have much fixedda rope, you can use." I refused. A second argument followed and I stated that I preferred retreat to using their ropes. How absurd. The fourth day on Fitz Roy, 35 pitches of hard climbing below us, starving and weak and I would not cheat. The Poles gave me strange looks and Bobby shook his head but finally responded. "If the summit means that much to you and you won't use their ropes, I'll try; but you'll have to do the hard leads." I felt inwardly happy, yet ashamed that we had to yell at each other about going to the top.

Steep, curving cracks disappeared swiftly beneath us and the pleasure of climbing on excellent rock softened my bad memories of our disagreement at the notch. Up above, the Poles shouted unintelligible words back and forth as they reascended their ropes. To them I surely appeared mad as I led strenuous pitches with a fixed rope dangling a couple of meters to one side. Fog, sun, hail and more fog brushed the mountain as we scrambled on rotten ice with ice hammers but no crampons. We met the Poles descending from the summit as we prepared to climb the low angled ice. They eyed us skeptically. I tried to tell them we had had to leave a few things behind in order to climb the North Pillar in four days.

Boulders appeared and the sought after views of the nearby peaks, especially Cerro Torre, awaited us. On these same slopes the French climbers Guido Magnone and Lionel Terray had plodded to the summit to make the first ascent 32 years earlier. Since then, members of 29 expeditions from Argentina, the US, Great Britain, New Zealand, Spain, Poland, Switzerland, Italy, South Africa, Chile and Japan had reached the top. Many of them had been exhausted and hungry like us; some had groped their way along to the summit in high winds. For us the air was calm but the summit view that meant so much to me did not exist. Clouds obscured all but Poincenot and patches of blue sky over the pampas. Bobby and I spoke hardly a word to each other. Although we had made the summit, it had lost its importance. I wondered what would become of our relationship and realized how selfish my decision to continue to the top had been. For seven weeks we had been imprisoned in a situation whose outcome might affect us forever. I hoped Bobby and I could live as friends.

Quietly we began to leave and at that moment the clouds parted for fifteen seconds, unveiling the rime coated spire of Cerro Torre. Shreds of mist floated across sheer walls caked with thick ice. The bulbous summit ice mushroom hung above the east face like a specter waiting for a fine warm day to loosen its great tonnage of frozen water. Three months earlier friends had asked if I would try to climb the Torre also. "It's too dangerous", I replied.
"With the high winds and the ice falling off, I wouldn't risk it." But the question pestered me and, after the phantom mountain had submerged into the fog again, I wondered.

Bobby and I spent two and half days rappelling down Fitz Roy and struggling through soft snow on the glacier to reach our snow cave. We were drained. For two days we lounged in the sun outside the cave eating and reading. Our friendship was intact; I was glad reaching the summit of Fitz Roy hadn't destroyed it. We talked of a coming expedition to Pakistan, and of more immediate plans to party with the Polish climbers when we all made it back down to the beech forest.

From the snow cave, Fitz Roy seemed exactly the same as it had been seven weeks before. The image of a beautiful and unattainable summit persisted. But something had changed. For a few moments Bobby and I had stood on the top, added our footprints to the snow and then left. Already the memory of the freezing bivouacs and incredible hunger had faded. I thought only of the brief view of Cerro Torre, and of all the climbers before us who had struggled to reach the highest point.

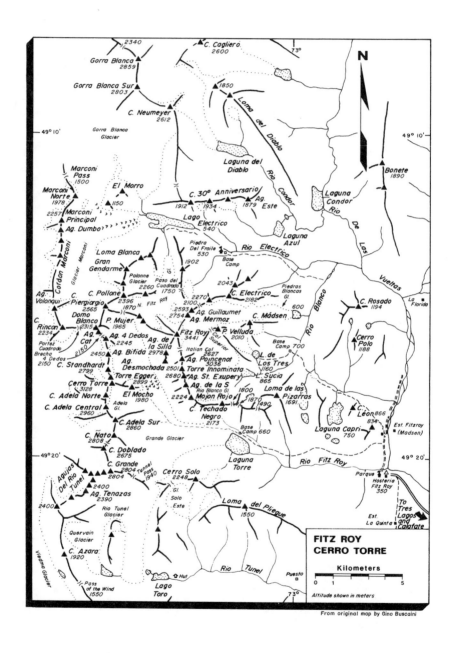

FITZ ROY
CERRO TORRE

Kilometers

0 1   5

Altitude shown in meters

From original map by Gino Buscaini

4

THE CERRO TORRE GROUP

The Torres

The three principal spires referred to as the Torres are Cerro Torre (3128 meters), Torre Egger (2900 meters) and Cerro Stanhardt (2800 meters). All three peaks lie a little over three kilometers southwest of Fitz Roy and are separated from it by a deep valley carved by the Torre Glacier. Francisco Moreno likely named Cerro Torre and Cerro Stanhardt on his journey in the late nineteenth century to determine the border between Chile and Argentina. Torre Egger was named after the Austrian climber Toni Egger by Cesare Maestri, in remembrance of his friend who died on Cerro Torre. Point Herron (2780 meters) is a subsidary summit of Torre Egger; it is named for the New Zealand climber Phillip Herron, who died in a crevasse fall. Cerro Stanhardt received its name from the German estancia owner Herr Stanhardt. The Torres rank as the most difficult Patagonian summits; the diminutive, but obstinate, Cerro Stanhardt remained a virgin summit until 1988.

Italian attempt on Cerro Torre: 1958

Cerro Torre sits on the edge of the Southern Patagonian Ice Cap and as a result the weather is even worse than on Fitz Roy. A deep gash, known as the Col of Conquest, separates Cerro Torre from Torre Egger to the north and the Col of Hope forms a saddle to the south, adjoining Cerro Adela. The ice cap flanks the west face of the mountain to within 1066 meters of the summit, but on the eastern side the Torre Glacier is another 450 meters lower. Above the Glacier, the east face soars for a kilometer and a half to the 3128 meter high summit. Although the spire is 313 meters lower than Fitz Roy, climbing it is no easier. When Terray compared Fitz Roy and Cerro Torre from a distance, he said of the Torre, "Now that, at least, would be worth risking one's skin for!"

The ascent of Cerro Torre is a dangerous undertaking and, when first viewed, the mountain seems to defy physical laws. In 1958 the Italian climber Carlo Mauri felt the objective hazards outweighed any rewards reaching the summit might provide. "The summit of the mountain looked like a giant cone that had been overfilled with ice cream and then pressed downwards, so that the ice cream spilled out further and further over the edges; but in the process of spilling, it had been frozen into immobility. As the west wind added more and more ice to the structure, it began to twist under the strain and distort itself into a crazy, upside down labryinth of ice, until gravity took over and blocks of ice the size of houses crashed down the smooth granite walls below." *Ice Sheathed Needle, Savage Fang of Rock*! and *Ice Frosted Granite Spire* are all names that the Torre has acquired over the years and each title unmistakably identifies the mountain.

Climbers had scrutinized photographs of the spire since 1936 and speculated on the possibility of making an ascent. In 1958 two Italian expeditions approached the peak, intent on climbing it. Bruno Detassis led his group up the Torre Valley and established a base camp near the outlet of Lago Torre. Upon beholding the objective, Detassis pronounced the Torre impossible and forbade his team to attempt it. Walter Bonatti and Carlo Mauri led the other Italian expediton. Bonatti was known for his many difficult ascents in the Dolomites and the Alps, especially his six day solo ascent of a new route (Southwest Pillar) on the Petit Dru. [I met Bonatti in Patagonia in 1988 and was impressed by his appearance. He was tanned and fit and, except for his snow white hair, looked as though he had just come down from attempting Cerro Torre. There were many questions I would liked to have asked him, instead I quizzed Silvia Metzeltin who was travelling in the same group. "Does Bonatti still climb?" "Oh yes! Unofficially that is. He won't use any modern equipment, not even a harness or the latest ice tools." Then Silvia laughed and said, "yet Bonatti still climbs better than we do!"]

In 1958 Bonatti and Mauri's expedition marched 64 kilometers to a camp on the ice cap below the West Face of Cerro Torre. Here they hoped to attack the mountain by its shorter and possibly weaker side. For a month they climbed and fixed six hundred meters of rope to the col between Cerro Torre and Cerro Adela. After waiting out storms at base they reascended the icy ropes on 2 February. The climbing had been moderate to this point but above them the Torre rose vertically for an additional six hundred meters to the summit mushroom. In places masses of ice overhung the route. Bonatti felt the climbing above the col was some of the most difficult he had ever experienced.

"We tied onto a four-hundred foot rope and began climbing directly towards the summit of the Torre. The ice was very hard for step cutting and so steep that at times it even exceeded the vertical."

The route was too difficult for Bonatti and Mauri who, later in the same year, would be the first ever to stand on the virgin summit of Gasherbrum IV (7922m) in the Karakoram. After leading up 120 meters on Cerro Torre, they descended to the col and down to the glacier. They named the cleft the *Col of Hope,* because they hoped to return to try the mountain again. Three days later the climbers made a north to south traverse of the adjacent Cordón Adela, completing first ascents of Cerro Adela and Cerro %ato; and making second ascents of Cerro Doblado and Cerro Grande. But the mountain tower did not yield. According to Bonatti, it might never be climbed.

Maestri-Egger ascent of Cerro Torre: 1959

When Bonatti and Mauri returned to Italy in 1958 and stated that Cerro Torre was impossible, most climbers were inclined to agree. Everyone but Cesare Maestri. He had been with Detassis the season before and believed the peak could be done. Maestri was called the *Spider of the Dolomites,* from his many difficult and solo ascents there. He returned to Patagonia in 1959 with the Austrian Toni Egger and Argentine Cesarino Fava. Egger was a well known ice climber who two years earlier had scaled the sheer East Face of Jirishanca (6126m) in the Cordillera Huayhuash, Peru. Fava had completed several expeditions to Aconcagua and Patagonia, including the attempt on Cerro Torre in 1958.

The trio approached the mountain up the bare ice and boulder studded Torre Glacier to establish a camp below the east face. Initially, Egger was out of action with an injured foot, so Maestri and Fava began establishing the route. For eleven days the pair anchored ropes and hauled food and gear to a height of 360 meters above the glacier and reached a feature they named the Triangular Snowpatch. While climbing with Fava, Maestri did all the leading and, according to Fava, it was well that he did. "From the way he (Maestri) climbs it looks relatively easy, he goes up about 150 meters, then tells me to follow him. I cling to the 12mm hemp rope which will remain fixed to the wall, do a pendulum swing to get myself over to a point beneath the vertical, and start. From the way I climb, belayed to Cesare, I am made fully aware of his extraordinary ability." But after climbing 360 meters, storms lashed the mountain and the climbers retreated.

Almost one month later, when the weather finally cleared, a transformation had taken place on the walls of the Torre. The smooth, holdless rock was caked in rime ice thirty centimeters to one meter thick. By now Egger's foot had healed and he joined Maestri and Fava for a second attempt. At Camp III, below the face, Maestri favored fixing additional rope above the Snowpatch before trying for the summit. Fava recalled Egger's feelings, "Toni, on the other hand, thought the best technique would be that already used

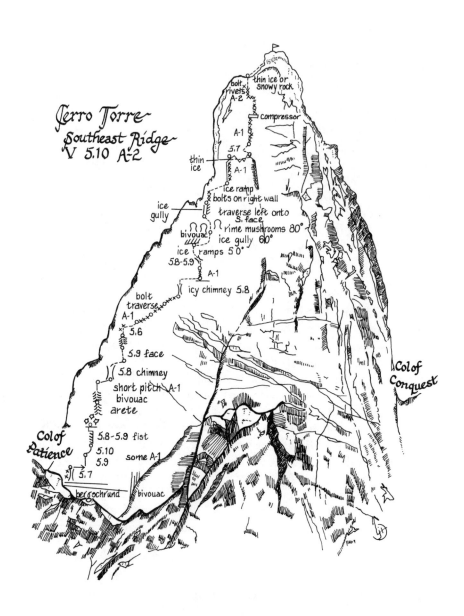

Cerro Torre
Southeast Ridge
V 5.10 A-2

thin ice or
snowy rock
bolt
rivets
A-2

compressor

A-1

5.7

thin
ice

A-1

ice ramp
bolts on right wall
traverse left onto
S. face
rime mushrooms 80°
bivouac
ice gully 60°
ice ramps 50°

ice
gully

5.8-5.9

A-1

icy chimney 5.8

bolt
traverse
A-1

5.6

5.9 face

5.8 chimney
short pitch A-1
bivouac
arete

5.8-5.9 fist

Col of
Patience

5.10
5.9

some A-1

5.7

bergschrund

bivouac

Col of
Conquest

on Jirishanca; to go up with everything we needed and be independent for five or six days. He said it would be quicker and less tiring." Egger persuaded the others to attempt a rapid ascent above the fixed ropes. Fava realized he would hold back the faster and more skilled pair, he agreed to carry supplies as far as possible in support and then return to Camp III. From the Snowpatch, the three climbers ascended on good ice to the *Col of Conquest* (so named later by Maestri). Maestri stated, "in the mountains 'hope' is a vain word, only the will to succeed counts. Hope is the weapon of weaklings." Fava descended and Maestri and Egger settled into their bivouac and prepared tea. The weather was stable and the night clear.

In the next two and a half days Maestri and Egger climbed 760 meters up steep ice and snow to the summit. The white substances hung precariously to the mountain and Maestri felt the entire surface could fall away, "At each step, the whole crust made a dull noise like a low whistle, it cracked and broke and large pieces fell off. The ice pegs went in like butter and gave us only an illusion of security. At each pitch we made a small platform, so that we could dig through to the rock, where we found not the slightest trace of a crack; so we had to drill holes for expansion bolts, and each hole needed five hundred hammer blows."

Maestri and Egger bivouaced a second and third time on the north face above the Col of Conquest. By the third bivouac they had climbed couloirs that led to just below the overhanging summit ice mushrooms. On the fourth morning the weather began to change as the two climbers battled their way through the final obstacles guarding the summit. As they reached the top a gust of warm wind blasted them from the west and heralded the end of the good spell they had enjoyed. They embraced each other, took several photos and started back down. Maestri felt the top was no place to tarry, "The summit was completely surrounded by cornices which threatened to break off at any moment. I climbed down over them without the least bit of emotion and without the slightest trace of disgust or fear." They reached their previous bivouac as the weather warmed even more and avalanches swept past them on either side. Through the night they huddled close and above the deafening roar of the wind Toni remarked, "Let's hope we don't die a white death."

On the morning of the fifth day they resumed the descent initially rappelling form bollards hacked in the snow. Lower down, the ice and snow had melted, revealing smooth slabs of crackless rock. Maestri described their descent, "We had to abseil down and hang on the end of the rope, while we drilled a hole for an expansion bolt for the next abseil. Finally, we bivouaced under a small mushroom, tied to expansion bolts."

Late on the sixth evening, Maestri and Egger descended from the Col of Conquest to just above the Triangular Snowpatch but were too weary to continue down the fixed ropes to the glacier. An avalanche swept Egger away as he searched for a safer bivouac spot. Depressed by the death of his companion, Maestri spent a cheerless night on the mountain and descended the ropes the following day. Within a pitch of the bottom, he slipped on a patch of verglas and fell to the base. Fava had given both climbers up for dead and was about to leave Camp III for Camp II when he spotted Maestri at the base of the wall. Fava led the delirious survivor the remaining distance down the mountain and later returned to search for Egger's body. Much snow had fallen since the accident and his remains were not to be found.

Lionel Terray called the ascent of Cerro Torre "the greatest climbing feat of all time." That was quite a compliment, coming from the man who first climbed Fitz Roy. But other climbers did not hand out praises so readily, especially Maestri's countryman Carlo Mauri who refused to believe that the pair had reached the summit. In an article about an attempt on the West Face of Cerro Torre in 1970, Mauri said, "the climber who succeeds in photographing the ice cream like formations on the summit will be able to say truthfully that he has gone beyond the limits of extrêmement difficile." Without saying Maestri had failed, Mauri referred to the

---

9. Cerro Torre, Torre Egger and Cerro Stanhardt from the east, below Poincenot. The first ascent route on Torre Egger (the middle spire) followed the lower East Face of Cerro Torre Egger *Nikon FM, 50mm lens, K 64*

10. Cerro Stanhardt from the southeast. Early attempts on this peak followed the diagonal ramp and buttress directly below the summit, and the great chimney on the right. The first ascent party in 1988 climbed across the ramp and up the narrow ice filled chimney in the center to reach the summit ridge and the top of the mushroom. *Nikon FM, 135mm lens, K 64*

11. Cerro Torre, Torre Egger, Cerro Stanhardt, Bifida, and Pier Giorgio from the southeast approach, a short distance from the Torre basecamp. *Nikon FM, 20mm lens, K 64*

12. North and West Faces of Cerro Torre from the Torre Glacier. Maestri and Egger followed the left side of the Face, just right of the shadows (their disputed route). The Italians in 1974 and the Americans in 1977 climbed the right skyline. *photo by Michael Bearzi*

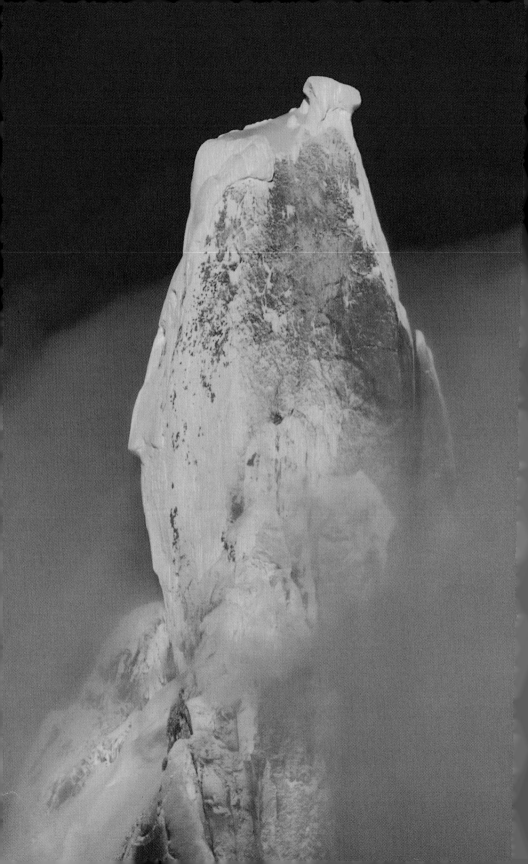

mountain as "unclimbed." Expeditions from Italy, Great Britain, Argentina, Spain and Japan also made attempts to climb the Torre and their failures fueled doubts about Maestri's and Egger's original ascent. Maestri's primary witness had died in the avalanche; and with Egger were gone camera and photographs as well. Perhaps, if the mountain were nothing more than a low angled, unattractive blob of snow, ice and rock, there would not have been such a fervor about who was the first to climb it; and to authenticate the ascent. But, according to *Mountain Magazine*, "It has become the epitome of the unattainable icy peak. This diminutive yet formidable mountain has come to embody the whole spirit of super alpinism."

Maestri and Egger had the ability to climb Cerro Torre, based on their previous experience and the mountain could have been caked with ice making possible a rapid ascent. The American climber Charlie Fowler met Cesarino Fava in Patagonia in 1978 and later stated, "Fava showed me pictures of Cerro Torre taken at that time (1959), showing much more ice than I've ever seen." The unanswered questions that climbers have raised are as follows: What was the climbing like and where did the route go on the face Maestri and Egger climbed? Could Maestri and Egger have ascended the route in the time Maestri said? Was the rock crackless beneath the ice and snow that cloaked the wall and did it require

---

13. East and North Faces of Cerro Torre from the Torre Glacier. Maestri and Egger climbed the shadowed lower East Face to the Col of Conquest; then up the sunlit North Face. *Nikon FM, 50mm lens, K 64*

14. Beda Fuster follows the first of four vertical pitches on the headwall leading to the summit of Cerro Torre. Austrians Hans Barenthaler and Manfred Lorenz sort their rope at the ice towers below as they prepare to follow. *Nikon FM, 20mm lens, K 64*

15. Mark Houston on Cerro Stanhardt; after reaching the chockstone on the north side, we spent an entire day climbing up to blank walls, then rapelling. In 1987 Cerro Stanhardt was still unclimbed. *Nikon FM, 20mm lens, K 64*

16. The upper five-hundred meters of the Southeast Ridge and headwall of Cerro Torre from the east at dawn. Maestri's air compressor hangs by three bolts in a small patch of ice in the center of the upper headwall. *Nikon F2, 600mm lens, K 64*

bolting? What evidence of belay and rappel anchors remained after almost two decades of bombardment by ice, rock and snow avalanches? Thus, the climbing world awaited the findings of the next expedition to follow Maestri's and Egger's line of ascent and descent.

Seventeen years later, Americans Jim Donini, John Bragg and Jay Wilson climbed Torre Egger, the spire next to Cerro Torre, following the Maestri-Egger route to the Col of Conquest. Donini was very experienced on big walls and smooth cracks, having honed his skills over many seasons in Yosemite Valley. John Bragg had superb free climbing ability from the Shawangunks and Jay Wilson, although only a climber of a few seasons, was mastering the sport quickly. The three found liberal evidence of hardware, rope shards and even rucksacks filled with gear to a point fifteen meters below the Triangular Snowpatch, beyond it nothing at all. Donini stated in an interview that all the crack systems and grooves on the lower portion of the East Face of Cerro Torre converge, leading to a hidden ramp which runs into the Col of Conquest. Donini said there was no other way to go that looked reasonable or logical. "You peek around the corner and there's a ramp system going into the Col about four hundred feet long, and that's where Maestri claimed that it was very difficult doing that traverse, and from below it looks like a blank wall, when in fact you turn the corner and there's a ramp that's easy, it's not hard at all ... from below you can't see the ramp."

In 1981 British climbers Tom Proctor and Phil Burke attempted Cerro Torre and climbed to within one pitch of the summit. Burke had substantial Patagonian experience from a 1979 attempt on the 1650 meter East Buttress of the Fortress. Proctor and Burke made an ascent of the east and upper north face of Cerro Torre and found difficult and nearly vertical climbing high on the north face. Maestri stated that this upper portion was around fifty degrees in steepness and not the seventy to eighty degrees which Burke and Proctor encountered. The British pair were thwarted by warm conditions; just below the top with Burke in the lead, "The ice was just overhanging mush, impossible to climb. I flayed with the now useless tools, stuck my arms in, udged up, but there was no purchase or traction." Given the angle of the summit overhangs, it is possible that the mushrooms would have overhung even more had the mountain been rimed up to the thickness Maestri said. The summit icecap is always changing, and photographs from 1971, 1985 and 1988 reveal different formations and amounts of ice.

Remembering the exact details of any ascent is not easy. Perhaps Maestri truly did not go the same way the Americans went or he recalled difficult climbing where it was easy and easy climbing where it was hard. A slight deviation or off route mistake on a mountain such as Cerro Torre produces extremly hard, if not impossible, climbing after only several moves. (It would be enlightening to question all climbers who have achieved incredible ascents but lack substantial proof. How will their stories hold up after many years have passed? Will they be able to describe the route and difficulties every step of the way?)

Could Maestri and Egger have made the entire ascent and descent in six days? A good portion of their time was spent placing bolts for belay and rappel anchors, since drilling in granite by hand is a slow process. Donini claimed the American climb of Torre Egger required six days just to reach the Col of Conquest. Since for them the rock was mostly bare, they had a number of aid pitches interspersed with free climbing, which made the route tedious. The trio continued to anchor fixed ropes the entire way up to the Col and dragged additional rope and hardware with them. They were not engaged in an alpine style ascent during that portion of their climb. If this section had a thick layer of ice and snow plastering it a fast ascent would be possible. This aspect of the 1959 ascent hinges completely on the condition of the mountain at that time.

The third question is whether the rock beneath the layer of ice and snow on which Maestri and Egger climbed was crackless and required bolts. Donini, Bragg and Wilson found the climbing up to the Col of Conquest to be "well protected and had good crack systems". The Americans climbed on rock relatively free of ice and snow except for ice back inside cracks and under those conditions the cracks can be more easily located. In 1985 I spent thirty minutes clearing away ice while searching for a crack on Cerro Torre and found nothing. It is likely that Maestri and Egger were forced to dig through the ice and place bolts if the ice varied from 25 centimeters to one meter thick. If, however, they were following obvious features such as corners, blocks, natural weaknesses and so forth they would know where to look for cracks. Placing pitons is much faster and easier than drilling bolts.

Finally, it is valuable to find out from subsequent expeditions what evidence remains in the way of belay or rappel anchors. Donini, Bragg and Wilson found nothing beyond the equipment dump just below the Triangular Snowpatch. Having personally witnessed what falling ice and rocks do to bolt hangers, sometimes shearing the hanger off completely and leaving a barely discernible six millimeter rusty stud, I wondered if this had occurred on Cerro Torre. In 1979 Don Peterson and Tom Bauman attempted to repeat the same route climbed by Maestri and Egger twenty years before. An aggressive Colorado climber, Peterson had gained notoriety from his ascent of Yosemite's Half Dome in 1969 with Royal Robbins. The same year Bauman completed the first solo ascent of the Nose Route on El Capitan also in Yosemite. Peterson and

Bauman found only evidence of the 1976 Torre Egger ascent above the equipment dump but nothing of older vintage. I asked Bauman if icefall could have eradicated the bolts from 1959, "Sure, but every single one? You'd think a few would have survived".

If the Torre were thickly plastered with ice, a rapid ascent by Maestri and Egger would indeed have been very possible. Did they really dig through the ice and rappel off bolts? Or did they chop bollards the entire way and leave slings which are long gone through melting and wind? Did Fava accompany Maestri and Egger all the way to the Col of Conquest and then rappel back down? Where are the anchors he used? What would he have to gain by saying he had climbed six hundred meters higher than he really had? Unfortunately, these are questions with no definitive answers. If Cerro Torre, even today, seems a compelling prize, imagine how it appeared to climbers in the late 1950's!

Southeast Ridge of Cerro Torre: 1968 and 1970 attempts

During the 1967-68 season Peter Crew, Martin Boysen, Mick Burke and Dougal Haston arrived from England to attempt the Southeast Ridge of the Torre. Argentine José Luis Fonrouge was asked to join the expedition because of his experience on Fitz Roy and his desire to climb Cerro Torre. Once in Argentina the expedition spent the first month sorting gear and carrying loads to a snow cave near the base of the mountain. During three clear, hot days in late December the climbers managed to fix six hundred meters of rope on the snow and ice face leading to the col. The weather remained clear and windy; on 3 January Fonrouge and Crew climbed a number of difficult rock pitches on the ridge above the col and fixed 240 meters of rope.

In the next several days the personnel changed and Burke, Boysen and Haston took over the lead climbing. The climbing became increasingly difficult and involved direct aid and even hook placements on the crackless rock. On 5 January Burke and Haston spent all day climbing only two pitches. Thus far the route they followed required conventional techniques, free climbing when possible and driving pitons for aid. But the higher they went the more blank rock cropped up. Crew wrote of their route choice in the final three hundred meters. "Our original plan had been to climb up the final wall (the headwall bolted by Maestri two years later) directly to the top but it was obvious now that this would take too much time. There were no continuous lines or cracks and it could only be climbed by very difficult artificial techniques."

What the British had hoped to do was climb the Southeast Ridge up to a point where snow ramps might lead around to the south and west faces of the mountain and thereby avoid climbing the sheer headwall. Once on the west side, they proposed to climb ice and snow gullies to the summit. The expedition encountered a serious problem at a point where the steep rock of the Southeast Ridge intersected the snow ramps. According to Crew, the lead climbers needed more bolts. "Easy ground lay only sixty feet away, but the intervening slabs proved to be too steep and smooth to climb free and there were no cracks for pitons. After seven hours of trying to climb this short section of rock, Boysen and Haston decided that they would have to come down and fetch another supply of bolts."

At that point the weather changed and pinned the climbers in base camp for 35 days. When they returned to the mountain to reascend the ridge, they found that the winds had tangled, frayed and even severed their fixed ropes. The expedition thus came to an abrupt end after twelve hundred meters of vertical climbing on the fifteen hundred meter route. They might have succeeded on their previous attempt had they not dropped their bolt kit or had extra bolts been readily available. In fact, the easier snow ramps the British climbers sought would have gained them only several pitches. No climbers have as yet traversed around to the west face; it is likely they would have been forced to climb the headwall in order to reach the summit. Many great ascents often owe their success to the groundwork, errors and toil put in by a previous unsuccessful expedition. The British mapped out the route up the Southeast ridge for the next group of climbers.

Subsequent expeditions rely heavily on such information to find the best route up the mountain. In addition, the newcomers are always keen to learn of any special equipment that might make the ascent possible. Choice of route and bolting were to become the key issues in the Italian attempt of 1970, led by Cesare Maestri. After learning of the British attempt and the blank rock that stopped them, Maestri chose a different method of attack. "It seemed to me that the route must be impossible by normal means, so I decided bolting would be necessary."

Maestri had claimed the first ascent of Cerro Torre in 1959 with Toni Egger but over the years criticism and doubts about his ascent had grown to a point where he felt action was necessary. Many climbers wondered why Maestri wanted to climb the mountain again. Maestri's response was, "Suppose you worked in a bank and, just before you were to retire, you heard a rumor that you had walked off with $20,000 of the bank's money, what would you do? Would you go to court and try to prove your innocence? Or if there was some way in which you could clear your name by one theatrical gesture, would you not choose that? Even if it involved a certain amount of danger to yourself, wouldn't you take the latter course?" He returned eleven years later with Ezio Alimonta, Carlo Claus,

Claudio Baldessari, Daniele Angeli, Juan Pedro Spikermann and Fausto Barozzi to climb the mountain again. To the disbelievers, he was saying, "This is what I can do, can you do any better?" Although he did not reach the top of the ice mushroom in 1970, he established one of the more challenging routes in the world. Of the two thousand meters of climbing (actual distance, not vertical height) on the Southeast Ridge, 350 meters are up bolts placed by Maestri. Many of the bolts were placed next to piton cracks but the majority of them are over crackless rock. Where bolts are absent, the free climbing on the mountain is of a high standard (see Appendix III) and numerous expeditions attempting Maestri's route since 1970 have failed to complete the climb, even when they used his anchors.

The peculiar aspect of the 1970 ascent is the means by which Maestri placed the bolts. He laboriously winched up the mountain a 68 kilo gas powered air compressor that supplied a pneumatic drill, not unlike the tool used to remove lug nuts from a car wheel. He felt it would simply speed up the process of drilling, which he anticipated would be considerable. But, instead of warding off persecution by other climbers, the skepticism became worse than ever. Articles from climbing publications attacked his ascent, saying, "he had beaten the mountain into submission and subdued it".

Maestri actually made two attempts to climb Cerro Torre in 1970, the first took place in the Patagonian winter. Maestri's words are a testimony to his determination to reach, for the second time, the ice encrusted summit that had eluded so many others. "For 54 days consecutively, we climbed on the smooth slabs and steep walls of the tower. Twenty-eight nights were spent in bivouacs. Most of the time we slept in hammocks, covered in drifting snow and buffeted by the wind. Of these 54 days, only six could be described as good; during the remaining 48, we recorded temperatures regularly between -20 and -25 degrees C, humidity between 80% and 90%, wind speeds never below 80 KPH with gusts to 150. In all, eighteen meters of snow fell over the period."

In 1987 I found remains of the wooden hut Maestri had had flown to the Torre Glacier by helicopter. After seventeen years, broken walls, half rotted boots and empty propane cylinders still lay scattered about. The refuse was a sad example of how littered mountains can become when climbers have mechanical assistance or many porters to help stock a base camp. When the trip ends, few remaining climbers have little incentive to remove the garbage. In 1972, the season after Maestri's climb, the American climber Doug Tompkins spent an entire day dumping the debris around the abandoned Italian hut into crevasses.

Maestri's expedition ran out of food 350 meters short of the summit on the winter attempt and he returned in the summer to finish the task. The fixed ropes were still usable and Maestri reached his high point, negotiated steep, mixed climbing on thin ice and reached the two hundred meter headwall. At this time the weather was good but they had mistakenly left most of their pitons below. Rather than lose their only chance at the summit, they utilized the compressor on the smooth headwall, about half of which could have been nailed with pitons instead of bolts.

The use of machines in climbing has always been controversial. On the East Face of Everest in 1983, rocket launchers and gas powered winches enabled climbers to trolly loads up steep walls. In Alaska, airplanes and helicopters have landed climbers at the base of mountains and sometimes plucked them off. In the late 1980s, two expeditions were helicoptered to the summit of Cerro Torre and then parapented off. In 1970 Maestri startled and offended climbers throughout the world with his air compressor. How handy Maestri would have found the present day cordless electric drill, in fact, several years ago an American climber considered taking a *Bosch Bulldog* drill to the Towers of Paine. To his credit Maestri nearly climbed Cerro Torre from the bottom up. He could have landed on the summit with a helicopter and bolted his way down. Nonetheless, critiscism of Maestri's tactics was severe.

In response to the objections to the compressor, Maestri stated, "We are inventing, let us say, a new brand of climbing, which will complement, not replace, the old. We are trying to carry climbing technique forward and by means of revolutionary techniques to enhance, not detract from, the human values of the sport, for the new techniques will render possible greater achievements requiring greater gifts of character and finer human qualities." In essence, Maestri was heralding "change", to which many climbers are resistant. Everyone's definition varies of what is a fair means of completing a climb. The compressor is one example of the extremes, thus far, by which climbers have utilized machines in the mountains.

West Face of Cerro Torre: 1974

The Italians had quite a stake in reaching the summit of Cerro Torre. After two attempts on the West Face in 1958 and 1970, they organized a third expedition in 1973 for the same route. A group from Lecco, led by Casimiro Ferrari, approached the spire as if it were a Himalayan giant, attacking the mountain with twelve climbers and hundreds of meters of fixed rope and ladders. At the time many climbers throughout the world still felt Cerro Torre had not been climbed to the summit. This would be an opportunity for the Lecco group to claim an indisputable first ascent of the mountain. With an inexhaustible supply of fresh climbers, a great deal of equipment and prior knowledge of the route and conditions, they greatly increased their chances of success.

For a month the climbers ferried loads from Estancia Túnel to base camp at 1609 meters on the ice cap. Their 64 kilometer trek was hampered by wind and knee deep snow. While the men were camping en route, a tent caught fire and flames incinerated valuable equipment and personal clothing. Then at base camp it rained so hard for two successive nights that water flooded their tents.

The Spiders (from the name of their climbing club, the Lecco "Ragni") established two camps above the ice cap, anchored ropes and stocked the tiny citadels with food, stove fuel, ropes, pitons and ice screws. The second of these camps was perched on top of a bizarre formation of rime ice named the Helmet. The ice plastered granite wall defending the summit towered 450 meters above the Helmet and made itself visible through the rare cloudless patches between storms. Where Bonatti and Mauri had labelled the route "impossible" in 1958, the Spiders of 1973 hoped to find a line through the maze of jutting ice formations and steep corners.

The lead climbers were looking forward to the moment they could begin the ascent up the solid ice and crumbling snow cornices above but, as always, the wind was dictating events. Ferrari watched the morale of the team wither.

"The next three weeks saw all our enthusiasm evaporate, day by day, slowly and seemingly irrevocably the wind began to pound us again, we soon came to realize that merely to resist for any length of time would require new moral fiber and reserves of strength. But nobody knew for how long we would have to do battle with this invisible enemy, more treacherous and more elusive than the peak itself."

On 6 January they fixed ropes halfway to the summit and then waited another week while the wind hosed the spire with snow and rime. Seven days later the wind eased enough to give the Italians their only chance. They started up. The climbing was intricate and strenuous as Ferrari, Mario Conti, Giuseppe Negri and Daniele Chiappa hacked their way through ice choked chimneys, up steep gullies and past bulges of rime ice. Access to the summit was blocked by thirty meters of overhanging ice, the only alternative was to traverse three rope lengths to the south and climb up a system of gullies and ribs. It was delicate work but at 5:45 pm on 13 January the four Italians reached the top.

Now the Torre had finally been climbed to the top of the mushroom. But where was the "proof"? They photographed the summit in the whiteout and nothing was visible but snow and fog. Despite the lack of photographic evidence, their ascent was recognized by the majority of climbers. Big expeditions had come and gone, leaving their mark on the Torre. It would be three more years before a small, lightweight group dashed to the top without relying on fixed rope or set camps.

First ascent of Torre Egger: 1976

Torre Egger is the middle spire of the three Torres and, at 2900 meters, it sits 228 meters lower than Cerro Torre. By 1976 two large expeditions had failed to reach the summit. In 1974 the British turned back because of huge blocks of ice that loomed above the route. The increasingly warm weather guaranteed that the sun loosened ice would eventually smite one of the climbing team. In 1976 a New Zealand group of nine climbers called off their trip when their youngest member Phillip Herron died from exposure after falling into a crevasse. Both expeditons found the climbing to be very difficult and the small, icy summit far from their grasp.

After the New Zealanders had failed on the East Face, a party of three Americans started up Cerro Torre's East Face hoping to ascend the South Face of Torre Egger from the Col of Conquest. John Bragg, Jim Donini and Jay Wilson arrived in the National Park in early December, rucksacks bulging with hardware and nearly eleven hundred meters of rope for fixing. Bragg and Donini had failed on Cerro Stanhardt the season before and were determined to reach a Patagonian summit. Expeditions trying a route of this nature are usually made up of six to ten climbers. There was a lot of load carrying and only the three of them to do it. Because of the uncertain weather and difficulty of the route, the trio planned to spend up to three months on the climb and stocked the base camp with that amount of food. They wanted to achieve the objective sooner than planned so that any remaining time could be used for sightseeing on the Atlantic coast. But the weather had other designs.

December and most of January were lost to bad weather and the climbers managed to fix only 180 meters of rope on the 1200 meter route. On 23 and 24 January they extended the fixed rope to the top of the Triangular Snowpatch, and a week later climbed three hundred meters higher during two good days. The line of ascent up the lower part of Cerro Torre was a dangerous one. Frequent storms coated the rock walls in ice; the longer the storm, the thicker the ice. When the weather improved, the climbers reascended their ropes. But the warm temperatures brought down the ice, damaging ropes and fraying nerves. Wilson was nearly hit by a two cubic meter block of ice while carrying a load. Luckily the missile collided with the rock and shattered into many smaller pieces a short ways above him.

The Americans continued diagonally up and right, following the Maestri-Egger line, and aiming for the Col of Conquest, the deep gash between Cerro Torre and Torre Egger. After two days of intricate aid climbing, free moves and cramponing, they finally reached the Col. Bragg, Donini and Wilson spent a miserable night at the Col and observed the signs of another approaching storm; wind, spindrift and swirling clouds. Down the fixed ropes they fled; over the boulders, across the ice and back over the talus slopes to their forest base camp. The three weary climbers did not return to the Col for two weeks, when they carried up a nylon and aluminum box tent. These rectangular structures, weighing between six and nine kilos, depending on the materials, sometimes afford solid protection against the elements. On 16 February the Americans' box was anchored just below the Col, for the next five days the climbers thrashed their way upwards over the most difficult terrain on the mountain.

The wall directly above the Col was overhanging and plastered with rotten ice. That route was unclimbable and the only option was to traverse right for two rope lengths, across steep ice covered slabs, to gain access to the summit above. Donini fell six meters on the slippery rock but managed to finish the pitch and set up a belay. Bragg led another traverse to below an eighteen meter section of overhanging blank rock. It was Donini's turn to lead again, he described what took place. "I got up to this point where I just couldn't go on. So I reached up and got in a three-quarter inch angle, a third of the way, and tied it off. Jay lowered me and I started to try and do this pendulum but it was so overhanging I couldn't touch the rock. So he ended up pulling me back and forth with the haul line. I ended up penduluming far enough to the right, getting a finger lock in this crack, and getting a pin in and clipping to it."

With Donini in the lead, Bragg and Wilson belayed and waited patiently as he spent three and a half hours surmounting the eighteen meter pitch. A lasso thrown over a pedestal of rock and the placement of one bolt saved the day. On the entire climb the three climbers placed only four bolts on the formidable route. Donini said, "We had some bolts with us but were real reluctant to use bolts. We always kept them way in the bottom of the pack so they were very hard to get to."

Above the blank wall and pedestal, the technical demands eased a bit. But warm weather made the going miserable and dangerous. The torrent of falling ice was constant and all around them, while water poured down the cracks and up their sleeves. The beginnings of a storm brought mist and sleet as the three anxious climbers continued fixing rope up difficult mixed ground to within 120 meters of the top. On 22 February they reascended ropes stiff from the cold and sheathed in rime ice. They had no idea what lay above, guarding access to the summit.

The ice and rock was steep, but climbable, and Bragg led up over verglas covered rock to within one pitch of the summit ice mushroom. The group was tense and very quiet. They were so close to succeeding. Donini's lead took him up to the ice mushroom where he ran out of rope. "Fifteen feet from the top I screw in this ice screw and it goes in that far (Donini held his thumb and forefinger three inches apart) and hits solid rock. And so I clean away a window looking for a rock anchor and it's obvious to me this is a monolithic piece of granite. The ice is just too thin to put real anchors in, so I yell down to John and Jay and they dig in the bottom of the pack, and there's the last of the bolts, and they send me up the bolt kit. And all I can remember is being on a awkward stance, windy and cold. It was hard, hard rock. It broke a couple of bits. I finally got in a single bolt, and they had to jumar on it."

Wilson climbed up five meters, traversed right to a low angled arête and went straight up to the summit fifteen meters higher. He shouted down to his companions through the storm and soon all three were huddled together on top. They left behind a carabiner they believed was Toni Egger's, congratulated each other and quickly began the descent. Neither the view nor the weather encouraged a lengthy stay on Torre Egger's icy summit.

West Face of Cerro Torre: Alpine style, 1977

In Patagonia, one can expect to spend months waiting for a good day that permits climbing. But once in awhile the ice cap is benevolent and hands out the rare treat of several continuous days of good weather. Even if the wind does not blow, laying siege to Patagonia's mountains with large groups of climbers, tons of supplies and spools of fixed rope cannot guarantee success. An expedition fixing hundreds of meters of rope might make some good progress while a group climbing alpine style just might reach a summit in a single lightweight push.

During the second week of January, Americans John Bragg, Jay Wilson and Dave Carman set out across the ice cap, with two weeks of food and gear piled on a makeshift sled, and arrived at the base of the Torre's West Face after two days. The skies cleared on the second day at base camp and the small expedition began their ascent. On the first day they climbed past the Col of Hope over moderate ground and gained the top of the Helmet, after negotiating several overhangs and a rotten snow chimney. While sleeping in the open that night, high cirrus clouds seemed to grow out of the star filled sky.

Bragg and Wilson led mixed pitches the next day as Carman stayed at the Helmet and hollowed out an ice cave for a more comfortable bivouac. The pair found the climbing difficult as they worked up a vertical chimney in a corner blanketed with rime ice and snow of varying consistency. Above the corner, an ice wall of ninety meters proved even harder and Bragg stopped leading late in the day as storm clouds obliterated the ice cap and buried the spire. Leaving their lead ropes fixed, they descended and joined Carman in the ice cave. Outside the wind roared for two more days.

As the storm waned, the skies cleared again and the wind dropped. The trio scurried up the chimney and fixed ropes, hoping to climb the remaining ninety meter wall quickly. Bragg spent three hours front pointing up a three to five centimeter layer of ice over rock, often resorting to direct aid with ice axe picks. Carman took the lead and soon discovered a natural ice cave that would serve as home for their fifth night on the mountain.

The fickle weather changed again and wind, snow and cloud flayed the wall. But the climbers were so close to the top the risk seemed worth it. The climbing was scary because of poor protection and tenuous holds on the crumbling rime and snow. At least the nine hundred meters of exposure below them was hidden in the storm. In a few more hours the group had climbed above a sea of clouds, the storm had broken. Above them the gleaming white ice mushroom of the summit hung in a flawless cobalt sky.

For two rope lengths the climbers traversed right beneath the summit overhangs and ascended a third pitch up a tight chimney. The vertical groove ended abruptly on a curious area of near level ice and snow fifteen meters in diameter. John Bragg, Dave Carman and Jay Wilson pounded each other on the back and hollered for joy. They had made the first alpine style ascent of Cerro Torre's West Face and were standing on that elusive summit.

Southeast Ridge of Cerro Torre: Alpine style, 1979

Nine years had elapsed since Cesare Maestri's ascent of the Southeast Ridge. Other expeditions had set foot on the Ridge but without success. More fixed ropes, hardware and detritus laced the walls of the Torre yet climbers returned home with a little more knowledge of the route and ferocity of the elements in Patagonia.

Skilled climbers of the late 1970's had climbed difficult alpine routes throughout the world in amazing times. The psychological barriers had begun to erode and the realm of the "possible" expanded. Three Americans arrived in Patagonia late in 1978 to climb Cerro Torre. One of them was Jim Bridwell. He was no novice on big granite walls, having spent years in Yosemite Valley, completing eight new routes on El Capitan and Half Dome and scores of difficult short climbs throughout the valley. In early 1978 Bridwell made the first ascent of El Mocho, below Cerro Torre and climbed a new route on Mojón Rojo across the valley. Just as in the previous season, Bridwell was having trouble getting anyone to climb the Torre with him. His two partners found little similarity between Patagonia and their native California. The quality of the granite corresponded to home but that was all; in a couple of weeks the pair left him to grapple with the weather and the mountain by himself. He didn't like the idea of soloing the mountain and so asked another American climber, who had just arrived in the Park, to join him. Steve Brewer was also keen to do Cerro Torre, although the spire was wrapped so tightly in a thick cloud he couldn't see the mountain he had agreed to climb. Bridwell acted the part of a salesman making a deal over the telephone. "It's a fantastic route," he reassured Brewer. "You lead the ice, I'll lead the rock and we'll climb this route in no time!"

In order to climb quickly the Americans had to pare down their gear, taking only the essentials. There would be no fixed rope, no established camps and no insurance should something go wrong. And in Patagonia a lot could go wrong. They haggled back and forth over which pitons to take, how many candy bars, five ice screws or six, sleeping bags or bivy sacs. They settled on two 9mm ropes, 25 pitons and nuts, 25 carabiners, six ice screws, a small bolt kit, jumars, slings, a Svea stove and cook pot, water bottles, candy bars, oatmeal and soup for three days, and sleeping bags.

Brewer dressed himself in layers of wool, pile and nylon, typical material for the climb. Bridwell had climbed in Patagonia two seasons before in 1977 and developed a different idea of what constituted appropriate climbing attire. Because the wind driven rain and snow had penetrated his expensive, breathable garments on the previous trip, he wore a neoprene skin diver's wet suit from head to foot. He felt it was preferable to be wet and warm rather than wet and cold. On Bridwell's first trip he met the British pair who climbed Poincenot. Alan Rouse said, "Bridwell walked into our campsite brandishing all sorts of space age equipment". Extreme climbs often demanded an extreme approach and sometimes revolutionary gear. In 1970 Maestri had climbed on the Torre with clothing lined with the reflective material used in space suits. Cerro Torre seemed to bring out the bizarre in climbing fashion and weaponry.

Bridwell and Brewer started up the six hundred meters of ice climbing on 3 January with bandoliers of ice screws and carabiners. Climbing is frequently compared with waging a war but climbers' attempts at inflicting physical damage on the mountain are puny. In reality, the peak is the one that holds all the ammunition and is not stingy about sending it down.

Throughout that day, ice dislodged by sun and wind pelted the ridge. The pair dealt with the ice face for several hours and had climbed six pitches up the rock when an icy chimney above them disgorged its contents. They ducked under an overhang as the torrent of translucent projectiles roared by. Further up the ridge the field grew thick with the scraps of previous battles. Brewer was amazed at the amount of gear former expeditions had left behind. "We encountered five or six clusters of hardware; clogs, pitons, rurps, cliff hangers, fifi hooks, ice screws, even clog ascenders, and carabiners; so many carabiners we couldn't use them all. Fixed ropes trailed from anchors, broken and shredded."

Judging by the debris, apparently somebody else had decided to make a rapid exit when the mountain pounded them unexpectedly with wind, ice and snow. It was not reassuring for Bridwell and Brewer to come across the abandoned gear, because it meant the owners had had serious problems on the route. But for them things went smoothly and they climbed rapidly until ten o'clock that night. Approaching darkness and their own weary bodies dictated a bivouac 1050 meters above the glacier.

Overnight the wind changed direction. A storm was moving in and in the morning the two Americans began climbing at a feverish rate, hoping it would carry them to the summit. Speed was everything. They raced up solid ramps of ice but slowed to a crawl when Bridwell encountered fifteen to thirty centimeters of ice encasing a line of bolts stretching for forty meters. Each bolt had to be cleared of ice before it could be used. He hacked his way slowly up the pillar and then accelerated again on the final headwall.

Three pitches up the headwall, Bridwell reached the air compressor and marvelled at the 68 kilo hunk of machinery hanging from the wall. The compressor and its small gasoline engine were encased in a curved metal sheath hung by a chain of doubled carabiners from three bolts. Just above the air compressor a row of broken bolts led to the edge of the ice dripping down from the shoulder below the summit. Here Maestri had eradicated his own route by breaking the bolts off with a hammer on rappel. No one is sure why he destroyed the bolts; perhaps he wanted to prevent other climbers from using his route or to prove that bolts were necessary to ascend Cerro Torre.

Bridwell re-established the route by drilling shallow holes for aluminum rivets, pounding in several pins and placing copperheads. From the last aid move, he free climbed delicately up smooth rock, reached the ice, put on his crampons and climbed up. Brewer soon joined him and together they quickly scrambled to the top of the mushroom. The wind raked the summit at ninety kilometers per hour, even though the worst of the storm had not yet arrived. Quickly, the happy pair rappelled to their bivouac site, ate, slept, and resumed the descent the following day. The full storm hindered downward motion on the third day. Frozen ropes, avalanches and the shrieking wind made rappelling and communication tedious. At the lower end of the bolt traverse Bridwell clipped into a bolt with a sling from his harness and yelled, "Off belay!" At that moment the sling broke and he went for a forty meter ride, slamming into the wall and breaking several ribs. Luckily he was still able to function and they both reached the glacier that day.

An incredible climb had ended; the tired climbers sipped tea and rum in the comfort of an Italian camp below Torre Egger. From the dregs of a disbanded expedition in December had come the sweet taste of success.

Cerro Torre: Solo ascent 1985

The odds of two climbers reaching the summit of Cerro Torre are slender and the chances of a single climber succeeding or even surviving are slimmer still. Another person on the rope can make the difference between life and death should an accident occur. A climber alone on the mountain can rely on only himself. Only the wind is his constant companion and frequent enemy. New Zealand climber Bill Denz made two solo attempts on the Southeast Ridge of the spire in 1979 and 1980. On his last try he reached the air compressor and climbed a short way above it before abandoning the climb in bad weather. Denz found the descent off the headwall exhilarating. "I threw the ropes out in the air, all they did was become a mass of spaghetti as the wind caught them. I started abseiling down. The ropes were hooked over flakes right and left of me, the rope was just a mess but then I found the wind was picking me up and throwing me back and forth across the face as I was rappelling, and this was quite an advantage, because I'd sort of swing with the wind and unhook the rope off a flake, and then swing back across the other side and unhook it off a flake there."

Denz had been away from base camp for nine days with only four day's food. He climbed higher than many groups of two and three and came to within eighteen meters of the top of the headwall below the summit mushroom. He sustained a long fall near the bottom while descending and retreated to base camp with an injured shoulder. In 1983 a French climber attempting to solo the mountain was not as lucky. Pierre Paul Farges had been gone from base camp a week when his body was found in a crevasse on the Torre Glacier. It appeared that a sérac had collapsed and swept him into the crevasse near the base of the Southeast ridge. He could have been returning from the summit but no one shall ever know.

In November 1985 the Swiss-Italian climber Marco Pedrini arrived in Patagonia to attempt a solo ascent of the mountain. Two years before he had climbed as high as the ice towers on the Southeast Ridge with Romolo Nottaris. The pair could not find Maestri's bolts under a one meter layer of ice and rappelled back down the ridge. With this previous knowledge of the route Pedrini planned to make a rapid solo ascent. The only way for Pedrini to succeed was by being extremely fit, technically skilled and by saving time not belaying on the climb.

Pedrini's first attempt ended 360 meters below the summit where strong winds stopped his progress. A week later he started back up the mountain as hot weather stripped the rock of ice and forced him to wear a tee shirt. Pedrini used rock shoes for much of the climbing, slipping plastic outer boots over them for the ice and snow. He climbed rapidly up the mixed sections and only on the more difficult pitches did the lone climber haul up his pack with a lightweight seven millimeter line. He had brought spare clothing, food and water but no bag or stove for bivouacing overnight. After twelve hours of continuous climbing, Pedrini reached the compressor around 7:30 pm. From here he belayed himself with a 9mm rope up the final aid pitch of the headwall, climbed up the backside of the ice mushroom and at 8:30 pm stood on the summit. For a few minutes, Pedrini lingered on top. As a full moon rose in the east, he began the first of 26 rappels back down to the Col of Patience and his snow cave.

Pedrini's achievement symbolized how efficiently an individual can move with very little equipment. A climber must attain a high degree of mental control and physical preparation to solo such a climb. Pedrini was killed one year later in the Alps when his rappel anchor failed while he was descending solo.

The first successful solo ascent of Cerro Torre by the Southeast Ridge was achieved with minimal gear and manpower and, brilliant as it was, could only have been accomplished by using Maestri's bolts. Cerro Torre, like many other great alpine faces in the world, has been the stage for two very different types of climbing. Each style has merits and faults and which path extreme alpinism follows will be determined by future climbers.

First Ascent of Cerro Stanhardt - 1988

The smallest of the three great spires that comprise the Torres is the squat Cerro Stanhardt. Although the mountain is one hundred meters lower than neighboring Torre Egger, and lacks Egger's steeple like appearance, it required eleven attempts by British, Swiss, Italians, Spanish, Argentines and Americans before yielding. One can gain a lot of elevation by climbing to the Stanhardt-Bifida Col on the north side, but from that point onwards the peak is deceptively hard, as the first expedition to attempt the climb in 1974 discovered.

Four climbers from Britain and the United States, Ben Campbell-Kelly, Brian Wyvill, Jim Donini and John Bragg, set up base camp in the beech forest above Lago Torre in November. Campbell-Kelly and Wyvill had plenty of mountain experience and had recently made the first alpine style ascent of the massive Troll Wall in Norway. Larry Bruce from the USA and Mick Coffey from the UK provided additionalsupport. The weather remained stable and Donini and Campbell-Kelly climbed two pitches above the Stanhardt-Bifida Col, traversed the highest ledge on the East Face and fixed two ropes in an ice glazed chimney that led to the summit ridge. Overnight the weather changed and their small bivouac on an ice ledge became a target for wind powered ice crystals. Donini retrieved the two ropes and the pair climbed back across the ledge and rappelled and climbed down to the glacier.

Storms enveloped the mountains for three weeks and clouds painted the skies a somber gray. On one trip from the col to base camp, the climbers discovered an old boot lying on the glacier. Wyvill described what they found. "Closer examination showed it to contain part of a leg and foot, further searching revealed other remnants of clothing and equipment." Donini stated, "There can be no doubt that it was Toni's body because of its position and the equipment, the boots made in Kitzbuhl." The climbers left Egger's remains on the ice, keeping only a carabiner to leave on the summit of Cerro Stanhardt.

On 1 January 1975 the expedition regained the high point but falling ice caused by the warm weather made the climb too hazardous to complete. Eight days later the four climbers tried again and got within fifty meters of the summit ridge after difficult and dangerous ice climbing in a huge chimney. Wet and freezing, they retreated in a storm and Stanhardt was neglected for two years.

British climbers Brian Hall and John Whittle were next on the scene, they made two attempts to climb Cerro Stanhardt by a slightly different route. In January 1977 the pair climbed to the Stanhardt-Bifida Col, then traversed the ledge on the East Face all the way to the Southeast Buttress of the peak. After a second bivouac, they did five pitches of hard mixed climbing to within 150 meters of the summit. Violent winds and snow forced them to abandon the climb; they waited seventeen days for another try.

Their second attempt was more productive; the two climbed to the Col and across the ledge and ramp in a single day. Leaving bivouac gear behind, on 10 February Hall and Whittle ascended ten pitches up the buttress using mixed climbing and direct aid. They stopped climbing near the top at 3 pm in deteriorating weather. Jim Bridwell was in Patagonia the same season and spoke with Hall and Whittle in base camp. According to Bridwell, they considered it a first ascent but admitted not climbing the final ice mushroom.

By now it should be apparent that the mushroomed summits in Patagonia are especiallly significant. The controversies about reaching the utmost top of Cerro Torre have established this precedent. Cerro Stanhardt's ice encrusted cap continued to repel humans for another eleven years.

In 1984 Swiss climbers Thomas Wüschner and Martin Mooseberger attempted the peak and failed one hundred meters below the top. Wüschner was also convinced that the British had not made the summit in 1977 which prompted him and Mooseberger to try it. Between 1984 and 1987, expeditions from Spain, Italy and the US were repulsed by Stanhardt's defiant walls. Another team of climbers would have to try to assemble the right combination of routefinding choices, logistics and talent to climb the spire.

In late 1987 an expedition from the US arrived to tackle the stubborn little mountain. Patagonian veteran Jim Bridwell brought along two climbers, Jay Smith and Greg Smith, with Elisa Moran in support. Jay lived in California and had plenty of Yosemite wall experience plus alpine credentials that included a first ascent of the North Face of Kang Taiga in Nepal. Greg was from Kentucky where he had honed his rock skills on the overhanging crags of the East and South. Together they possessed a keen knowledge of the area and excellent technique for any conditions.

By December the group had fenced with the weather and made several stabs at reaching the mountain. In a moment of weakness, the weather allowed them to climb to the bergschrund below the Stanhardt-Bifida Col and bivouac. That evening Jim and Jay fixed their lead ropes above the schrund and returned to the icy hole for dinner.

They had planned on a civilized breakfast before starting up but were alarmed to discover two Argentine climbers already on the slope and climbing up their fixed ropes. This dampened the merriment of the morning and it would not have consoled the Americans to learn that Sebastian de la Cruz and Peter Spiri had amassed no less than four ascents of Fitz Roy.

Luckily each party had a different route in mind and a confrontation involving many sharp instruments was avoided. The Americans veered off and followed in the footsteps of Hall and Whittle, hoping for an ascent of the Southeast Buttress. The climbing was hard, the weather went bad and the despondent trio descended. Time passed (as it eventually does, even in Patagonia) and the climbers returned to the mountain on 28 January.

This time Bridwell and the Smiths ascended unroped to the Col using a direct start and tied in before negotiating the slabs above. Tedious climbing across bare rock and thin smears of ice and snow took all afternoon and into the evening. The three chose a bivouac site between the two great gashes on the east face. The first chimney was the scene of the 1975 attempt and contained rotten basalt rock and skimpy ice. The second chimney closer to the summit contained thicker ice but was tilted at an absurd angle. This would be the route of their ascent in the morning.

In the dawn light, the gigantic, ice choked crack was more intimidating than the night before. Bridwell described the scene. "A twisted elevator shaft soared upward, glistening at the back. A narrow wall of glass bulged and curved ever so curiously, precluding the complete view. What we could see was a test indeed, but that which is hidden is always the most frightening, the ever unknown."

For the entire day the three hacked their way up the glass bulge for six pitches. The first four leads were the most demanding physically but, like all frozen waterfalls, the climb had that impending feel of insecurity and transience. Would it still exist the next day? Or would it fall off?

Close to dusk, the exhausted climbers wormed their way up through the vertical rime ice leading to the very top of the summit mushroom. They were elated and for good reason; not another human had set foot on that spot. Not a single bolt or line of fixed rope marred the ascent, which made their success that much sweeter. For thirteen years Stanhardt had put up a good fight and, though the mountain has been scaled, its walls glisten with challenges for the ambitious.

5

ON CERRO TORRE'S SOUTHEAST RIDGE - 1984

Two weeks after climbing Fitz Roy in 1984, I hiked to the hut near Cerro Torre for a few days of relaxing and photography. I still hadn't gained back any of the weight lost on Fitz Roy; I felt weak. I had just leaned my pack against a tree when a tall energetic man, with dark curly hair, ran out of the hut and asked me if I wanted to climb Cerro Torre with him. His name was Beda Fuster; he was Swiss and had climbed many difficult routes in the Alps, Alaska and the Himalaya, including the Eiger North Face. I did not immediately reply, but set about fixing a large dinner; asking Beda questions about his climbing techniques and experience.

I learned that Beda had planned for many months ahead to climb Cerro Torre, but a few weeks before their flight to Argentina his partner backed out. Beda travelled from Switzerland anyway; in hopes of finding another climber, or of soloing the mountain. I was neither unfamiliar nor unsympathetic with his situation but, in order to climb Cerro Torre with Beda, I needed a vitality injection and a strength restorative. I was tired. He said to me with clenched fists, "I have so much energy for this mountain, I must climb it!" "Great," I thought, "you haven't already endured seven weeks in Patagonia, frosted your toes in two sleepless and foodless bivouacs on Fitz Roy, climbed seventy pitches and performed sixty-five rappels in two attempts. Energy is not something you just pull out of a bag."

Each day more climbers hiked to the Torre hut and took up residence. One zealous German climber was chopping wood furiously, no doubt to keep his arms from getting soft. "They are like this when they first arrive", I said. Beda translated my observations to the German. His reply was, "I always have energy." After the German's first attempt and failure on Cerro Torre with his two companions a week later, he was no longer full of energy. He began to talk of other places, his mind no longer focused on the fifteen hundred meter icy shaft. At the end of January his friends climbed the mountain without him. Many climbers turn back on the Torre, I wondered whether I would fare any better.

By now I realized that Beda held the same drive as I for Fitz Roy, and the same frustration when he no longer had a partner. I knew I was taking a gamble by joining a stranger for one of the most serious climbs of my life, but I felt lucky. When I finally agreed to accompany Beda on the climb, I still couldn't indulge in a good rest because my climbing equipment was stored in a stable eleven kilometers away. I hiked down for the gear and returned to the hut the same day. Inwardly I was thankful to see a week long spell of good weather come to an end, so that I could remain inactive and eat.

A storm had settled over Cerro Torre, Torre Egger, and Cerro Stanhardt; Beda and I turned our attention to "working", with a rigid schedule of baking and cooking every day. The smells of fresh baked bread, enchiladas, pizza, biscuits, cookies, cake and pudding filled the hut. The cooker burned deadwood so we were kept busy collecting branches from Magellan beech trees knocked flat by the winds. In places, stumps of green trees indicated that not all climbers had shared our respect for the forest. Plastic and paper littered the ground, creating an unsightly carpet of orange, black and white refuse. The same climbers who foul the forests practice their untidy habits on the mountains. Some believe the wind will blow their garbage away but most are just too lazy to carry it down. Beda and I kept ourselves busy picking up trash, but after three weeks we were becoming anxious to climb the mountain.

A day finally arrived that was good enough to attempt the Torre. There was no sign of wind, a minimum of clouds swirled about the peaks, and the barometer gave the highest reading yet. We spent the day hiking over the talus slopes, crossing the Torre Glacier and climbing six hundred meters of snow, ice and rock. We reached the Col of Patience, a flat area of snow the size of two large swimming pools, cradled between the snubbed summit of El Mocho and the spine of the Southeast Ridge. It was given the name by a member of the 1968 British expedition that spent many days in a snow cave waiting for good weather. Above the Col, the Southeast Ridge rises in an elegant curve toward the ice towers, the sheer headwall and the summit. The Col is the last place a climber feels the security of solid ground, without terrific exposure on three sides. I was reluctant to leave this place of relative comfort; I fiddled with my bootlaces to kill time.

As always, Beda exuded enthusiasm; hesitancy did not seem to be a part of his personality. I began to understand how Bobby had felt on Fitz Roy only one month before. In the remaining light we rapidly climbed five pitches up difficult cracks and snow covered rock to a tiny ridge of snow. Just at dusk, we excavated a one by two meter ledge in the snow, then laid down the rope and our pack for insulation. I snuggled into a lightweight synthetic bag and a bivouac sac while Beda covered himself with only a nylon sack. To save weight, he had refused to bring a sleeping bag; he had insisted, unsuccessfully, that I do the same. After Fitz Roy, I couldn't again face being cold several nights in a row; I knew Cerro Torre would have even lower temperatures. The day had been strenuous; all I wanted was a bite to eat, a hot drink and sleep.

Our butane stove coughed in the breeze as nuggets of snow melted into the precious water we craved. I poured a half liter of boiling water into a freeze dried dinner, let it soak five minutes, then rapidly devoured the meal. My stomach did not agree with the instant food; in a few minutes I lost everything. Beda handed me a 100 gram bar of Swiss chocolate in a red wrapper.

"The Swiss make the best chocolate and this is the best Swiss chocolate." He emphasized the word "Swiss." It did taste good, and it stayed down. Stars twinkled in a clear sky; after pounding flat a couple of annoying lumps of snow beneath my bed, I fell asleep.

Morning brought a blanket of dark grey clouds that neatly covered the summits of Fitz Roy and Poincenot. My stomach tightened as I imagined trying to rappel the Southeast Ridge in a storm; it worried me that clouds had materialized so quickly. We ate a breakfast of hot cocoa and bread that Beda had baked in the hut. I was still weak from losing my dinner the night before. Beda wanted to take the lead, thinking I would be too slow and almost useless. Perhaps he was right. However, I hadn't joined him only to pay out the rope while he led the entire climb.

Once moving, I felt better. The climbing was excellent. A short aid pitch bristled with fixed pitons and led to mixed ground below a squeeze chimney. Small icicles clung to the walls as I placed stoppers and clipped into old pitons. At the chimney top, I cleaned the cracks of powder snow to arrange belay anchors, then shoved my aching fingers into my parka to rewarm them. Beda led a pitch of steep flakes, then we each led more mixed climbing up coarse granite with patches of ice and snow. Beda's lead up rock covered with thin ice ended at a belay garnished with faded ropes, a harness, pitons and carabiners from previous expeditions.

From the belay I started a diagonal pitch, climbing free next to the bolts Maestri's had placed in 1970 with his gas powered air compressor. Soon the wall steepened; we spent several hours using the bolts for direct aid in a long rising traverse. The traverse appeared to be an awkward place to descend; the purpose of the threadbare and faded fixed ropes puzzled me. Beda tackled an ice coated chimney; I could hear his crampons screech as their points scraped rock. I did a short steep pitch up a bolt ladder, then Beda clawed his way up a flaring, off width crack dusted with powder snow.

Late in the afternoon we approached fifty degree ice ramps as the clouds unzipped, pouring out snow and fierce winds. In 1979, Don Peterson had come to climb Cerro Torre with Tom Bauman. Before the pair departed for Patagonia, I asked Peterson if he was excited about the trip. "Yes, terribly. I love the wind! I love the wind! I love the wind!" he howled, pounding his fist on a table.

Twenty-six pitches up on the Torre, I tried Peterson's reassuring chant but without success. Instead, tiny pieces of ice driven at high speed stung my mouth and drowned the words. The situation approached absurdity as I cramponed up to Beda's belay on the ice. I indicated the stupidity of continuing our ascent. He suggested we go a little higher; because the climbing looked appealing and it was my lead, I agreed.

For more than ninety meters I worked up perfect ramps of rime and water ice, then through a gully, and finally nine meters up fragile rime to a bivouac site. Huddled beneath a red bivouac sac were two Austrian climbers, Hans Barenthaler and Manfred Lorenz. They had been slightly ahead of us for two days, it was good to finally catch up with them and share stories over hot tea. Hans did all of the leading on their climb as he had the experience of difficult Himalayan and European ascents, while Manfred's money financed the trip. The evening's discussion focused on the weather.

Wind whipped the ropes about. Everyone agreed it was wise to have stopped at 7 pm, and to wait until morning to assess the situation. Visibility dropped to twenty-five meters; a hispid growth of rime the size of tiny worms began to form on our clothing. Our perch between several steep gullies grew more bizarre with each passing hour. Ice feathers sprouted from the wall as violent gusts of wind tore at my bivouac sac. I clutched the fabric more tightly and fussed with the butane stove to produce hot drinks and dinner.

Our ledge was cut from a wall of rime and water ice, it measured only 60 x 120 centimeters. Ice screws, pitons, stoppers, *Friends*, hammers, crampons and our ropes hung in clusters all around us. After dinner, I hacked furiously at the ice to enlarge our seat; Beda maintained the ledge was adequate and remained in his sac. Our tolerance for discomfort differed in many ways. I felt sure the ledge was too narrow, that I would peel off during the night, to end up three meters below hanging by the rope. The bivouac was no place for loose bodies or climbing gear. So far, Beda had dropped a mitten, an étrier and his headlamp; I insisted he clip everything into slings, including my pack, which he used for a pad.

Our situation both fascinated and frightened me. So long as no one moved we were secure, but we had no idea how much stronger the storm would get or how difficult it would be to go up or down. Right then I did not want to be on Cerro Torre. I craved the boring days and nights in the Torre hut where the biggest decisions involved choosing what to cook for dinner and how many guests to expect. If this was what I had to endure to climb the mountain, then it wasn't worth it. I didn't give a damn what people would say when I returned home after failing. All I wanted to do was crawl down into a hole on flat ground and pull the sod over the top. I slept only thirty minutes that night.

On our third day the sun came out and the wind dropped to a breeze. The intense storm seemed to have dissipated, though there were still shreds of harmless clouds around the mountain. The day was fine for climbing, in several hours Hans, Manfred, Beda and I ascended firm ice and two bolt ladders to the base of the headwall. I led directly above the ice towers on vertical flakes, the only pitch of free climbing on the headwall. My fingers curled over smooth wafers of granite as I stuffed *Friends* in for protection. Ice filled the cracks but the flakes were dry and the moves exhilarating.

The tips of the ice towers rose thirty meters above the fog; below us the ant like shapes of Hans and Manfred traversed across the gleaming rime. Swirling clouds hid the glaciers, Fitz Roy was seldom visible and the upper 180 meters of the Torre stood alone. On up the bolts we climbed towards Maestri's compressor. A steel *come-a-long* and eighteen meters of cable provided the answers as to how Maestri had winched the compressor up the wall; all of us became speechless at the sight. I couldn't resist touching the metal casing that enclosed the compressor and gas engine. The cold steel gave no indication it had ever been capable of delivering power to an air drill. No doubt the air rang many times with Italian profanities when the little engine failed to start or the starter rope broke! Any climber who reaches the compressor is very close to the summit; the atmosphere becomes even more subdued as each person hopes to avoid any little mistake that could keep him from the top.

Beda climbed above the compressor and stepped gingerly into rotting bits of perlon attached to Bridwell's rivets. As the rivets ended, Beda climbed for nine meters up over smooth snow covered granite to firm ice. The fine weather we had enjoyed most of the day came to an abrupt end. Cloud streamers moving at high speed again wrapped the four of us in white gloom. Windblown rime from the mushroom started to bombard me as the fresh and unexpected storm screamed at the mountain. I was not going to retreat that close to the summit; in another 45 minutes I reached Beda's belay on the shoulder and groped my way across gentle snow toward the highest point. In three directions the edge of the mushroom fell away into a cloud torn void fifteen hundred meters deep. Beda wore a huge smile as he staggered my way in the fearsome gale. Hans and Manfred, only minutes behind us, also reached the top but we held off any rejoicing or backslapping until later.

The descent was wretched. We had to cut thirty meters from our ninety meter rope when it hung up on our third rappel. The wind tore at us from every side, our eyelids periodically froze shut, and the sleeve on my locking carabiner kept freezing open on rappel. Descending the bolt traverse was the worst. For speed, we chose to rappel instead of climbing down the bolts; we clipped a carabiner and runner to the old frayed fixed ropes. Using the fixed ropes as a handline prevented an accidental thirty to sixty meter pendulum into the nearby wall. At midway points where the ropes were knotted to bolts, we had to unclip the sling and carabiner while rappelling, then clip it into the rope below. After rappelling for a day and a half, we all reached the Torre Glacier safely.

When Beda and I unroped after descending the glacier, I felt the tension between us disappear as though an electrical switch had been flipped off. My lesser enthusiasm had dampened some of the joy Beda felt for the climb; in turn his pushing me had been stressful. The relationship between Bobby and me had grown stronger after Fitz Roy; by continuing to communicate, I hoped Beda and I would do as well. Just then I was so tired that even talking required too much effort.

The last of my energy seeped away, leaving a vacuum into which relief flooded. Hans, Manfred and Beda hurried back to the hut as I stumbled along, barely aware of the pain in my body or of my own achievement. To have climbed either of those incredible mountains was a dream fulfilled. To have climbed both on a single trip was more luck than I deserved. Stars again dotted the night sky; the storm that could have lasted many weeks simply vanished. I finally reached the hut at 1 am and fell asleep on the bench inside without a sleeping bag. Two German climbers woke me at 7 am, as they fixed breakfast before heading out to climb Cerro Torre. I ate the piece of fudge they handed me, wished them luck, then fell back into a deep sleep.

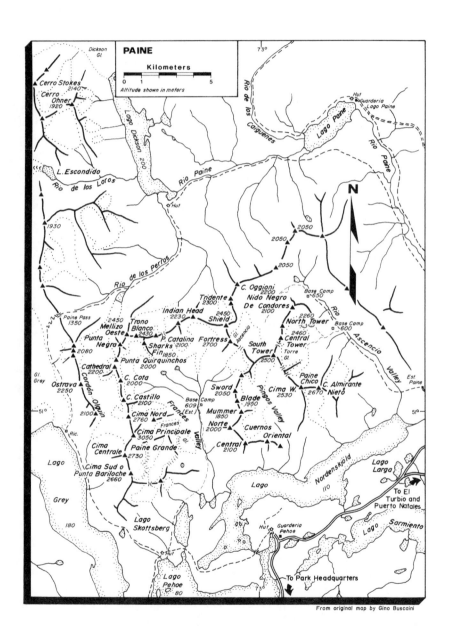

6

THE PAINE GROUP

The Paine Massif

One hundred and ninety kilometers south of Fitz Roy, in Chilean Patagonia, there rises a smaller cluster of granite spires called the Towers of Paine. The word "Paine" means "sky blue"; it was first applied to this region in 1886, when an Argentine traveler in southern Chile noted the similarity between the Chilean peaks and mountains in Argentina with the same name. As with Fitz Roy and Cerro Torre, the Paine is bordered on the west by the southern Patagonian Ice Cap and on the east by the pampas.

The compact range of peaks is split by three major river systems from east to west; the Río Ascencio, Río Pingos and Río Francés. Paine Chico (2670 meters), the South (2500m), Central (2460m) and North Tower (2260m) of Paine lie on a south to north axis and are flanked by the Torres Glacier on the east and the Ascencio Glacier on the northwest. Both glaciers drain into the Río Ascencio and then Lago Nordenskjöld. Slightly southwest of the three Towers are the Sword (2050m), Blade (1950m), Mummer (1850m) and Cuernos del Paine (2100m). On a north-south axis, these peaks are bordered by the Pingos Valley to the east and Francés Valley to the west. A cirque wall forms a pass at the head of the Ascencio Valley, separating it from the Francés Valley.

From the pass, the western portion of the range forms an inverted **L**. The Fortress (2700m) lies at the top and eastern end of this **L**, and is flanked by the Ascencio Glacier to the northeast. North of the Fortress is the Shield (2450m) with Shark's Fin (1850m) and Catedrál (2200m) to the west. From Catedrál, Cerro Castillo (2100m), Paine Norte (2760 meters) and Paine Grande (3050m) stretch to the south. Below the East Face of Paine Grande, the Francés Glacier is actively scouring away the unstable rock.

The peaks receive less moisture than Fitz Roy and Cerro Torre; the spectacular ice mushrooms capping the summits are either absent or much smaller, with the exception of the Fortress and Paine Grande. Wind blows constantly; the Italian climber Armando Aste claimed the wind blew harder in the Paine than further north. Climbers mistakenly believe that blue sky indicates fine weather with no wind.

Pilots flying the mail along the Argentine coast in the 20's and 30's discovered the hard way that clouds or an obvious storm front do not always accompany the wind. These brave souls flew in open cockpit biplanes; they often recognized high winds from a distance by a grey blue tint in the atmosphere. Experienced pilots tightened their harnesses and fought desperately to keep their five hundred horsepower craft under control. On rare occasions the mail planes flipped over and blew out over the Atlantic Ocean, far from land. Unlucky pilots disappeared at sea when their fuel ran out.

Antoine De Saint Exupéry flew the Patagonia mail during those years. In his book, ***Wind, Sand and Stars,*** he wrote about the sky and his feelings minutes before his plane was engulfed by the wind on a flight from Trelew to Comodoro Rivadavia. "The sky was blue. Pure blue. Too pure. A hard blue sky that shone over the scraped and barren world while the fleshless vertebrae of the mountain chain flashed in the sunlight. Not a cloud. The blue sky glittered like a newly honed knife. I felt in advance the vague distaste that accompanies the prospect of physical exertion. The purity of the sky upset me. Give me a good black storm in which the enemy is plainly visible."

Exploration

Paleontology, not climbing, initially attracted scientists to an area 56 kilometers south-southeast of the Paine Towers. In 1895 Hermann Eberhardt, a German sea captain, discovered giant bones in a cave at the head of Last Hope Inlet. The discovery came to the attention of Argentine paleontologist Florentino Ameghino and British Professor E Ray Lancaster. Ameghino and Lancaster identified the bones as those of the mylodon (giant ground sloth), an extinct ice age mammal. Further discoveries led the scientists to believe that prehistoric man had domesticated the mylodon, thus prompting expeditions to search for live animals, but without success.

Father Alberto De Agostini arrived in Punta Arenas in 1909 to begin his work as a missionary. Among his twelve expeditions to explore and map Patagonia, he made one trip to the Paine Towers in 1929, adding much to the knowledge of the area. A pair of German alpinists, Stefan Zuck and Hans Teufel, arrived in Patagonia in 1937 and made first ascents in the Darwin Group of Tierra Del Fuego, far to the south of the Paine. Moving north, they entered the Río Ascencio Valley and camped below Paine Chico, which is capped by a decomposed heap of black slate. Teufel and Zuck made a one day ascent up the broken rock of the 2669 meter mountain's Northeast Ridge. They climbed the eastern summit (Cerro Almirante Nieto) of Paine Chico and looked westwards to a range full of alpine wealth, glittering on the horizon. Sixteen years later the treasure seekers arrived.

Paine Grande: Attempts in 1953, 1955 and 1957

Rising to a height of 3050 meters, snow and ice clad Paine Grande is the highest peak in the range. The ice cap is only four kilometers to the west and the mountain's east wall of snow, ice and crumbling rock falls 2400 meters to the Río Francés Valley. In December 1953, a group of Argentine climbers attempted the peak from the south but found no easy route and experienced only two good days of weather in a month. Late in the season, the expedition got a short distance up but an avalanche broke off a hanging glacier, swept the face and buried Heriberto Schmoll and Tonchek Pangerc. Their bodies were never found.

The following season, Otto Meiling and Augusto Vallmitjana studied the western cliffs and reached a height of 2286 meters below the col separating Paine Grande and Paine Norte. In January 1955 an expedition of Chilean climbers, led by Eduardo Meyer, got to within 120 meters of the same col; bad weather and vertical rock smothered in snow prevented them from reaching the summit. Two years later, in November, Argentine climbers Carlos Sonntag and Davorin Jereb climbed for eighteen hundred meters up snow and ice to the base of a steep rock band just below a snow gully but ran out of daylight and descended the face. The pair returned two days later, climbed the rock to the snow gully and then retreated in deteriorating weather without reaching the summit.

Paine Grande and North Tower: First ascents 1957-58

In late 1957 an Italian expedition, organized and led by the millionaire Count Guido Monzino, made the first ascent of Paine Grande up the route pioneered by the Argentines the previous month. Jean Bich, Leonardo Carrel, Toni Gobi, Camillo Pellissier and Pierino Pession climbed for six-and-a-half hours above the last of the Argentine pitons on 27 December, to stand on the highest snowy pinnacle of the peak.

After establishing a new base camp in the Río Ascencio Valley in January 1958, Bich, Carrel, Pellissier and Pession tackled the sheer south ridge of the North Tower (2600m). The ridge rose eighty vertical meters above the col between the North and Central Towers before easing off. On 10 January the four Italians prepared the lower portion of the route leading to the col between the North and Central Towers. This section involved primarily snow climbing up a long couloir and several pitches of rock to the col. The climbers reached the notch at 1 pm, then anchored fixed ropes over the hardest parts before descending. Bad weather set in and the group did not return to the mountain until a week later.

Toni Gobi and Gino Barmasse joined the four original climbers and the entire party climbed to the col by 7 am on 17 January. A snow squall and wind threatened to halt their ascent but they decided to push on. Three steep pitches rose above the col; according to Bich, "these were the hardest, as the wall was very polished, without holds, almost without fissures. It required four hours of effort and the use of two hundred pitons and an imprecise number of étriers. After this first section the difficulty diminished; the snow, however, was very troublesome and made everything very slimy."

The climbers reached the false summit by late morning and traversed one long rope length to the base of the summit pinnacle. At first glance, the final 21 meter tower looked impossible. Upon examination the Southwest Face revealed a line of holds barely visible on the shadowed side. Here they climbed up fragile flakes on the near vertical wall and reached the top at 12:30 pm.

The first of the three striking Towers had been ascended; news of the enticing walls of sparkling granite soon reached other European climbers.

First ascent of the Central Tower: 1963

The almost flawless pillar of brown rock rises twelve hundred meters above the Torre Glacier, on a clear day the mountain is visible from 160 kilometers away. In 1962 a group of seven British climbers felt the unclimbed spire was worth fighting for. They wanted to be the first to climb the Tower.

Chris Bonington, Vic Bray, Ian Clough, Dr. Barrie Page, John Streetly, Derek Walker and Don Whillans arrived in November at a ranch sixteen kilometers from the mountain's base. Whillans and Bonington were the most experienced climbers in the group. Whillans had made the first ascent of Aguja Poincenot in 1962. Between 1957 and 1961, Bonington had scaled the Bonatti Pillar and the Central Pillar of Frenêy in the Alps, and Annapurna II in Nepal. At Estancia Radic, the British expedition poured out of two Chilean army trucks in a stream of empty beer bottles and dust. Frazzled by dealing with inquisitive border guards and bumpy roads, the sight of the mountains reassured the weary travellers. The group hoped the skies would remain calm for the climb but were piqued to learn from the local ranchers that a month of perfect weather had just elapsed. Whillans asserted that, if this information were true, they could expect a lot of rotten weather in the forthcoming weeks. Windless skies never lasted very long.

Slowly the expedition members lugged several tons of equipment up the densely forested Río Ascencio Valley to a position close to the mountain. An examination of the Tower's various facets revealed low angle rock slabs, rising three hundred meters to a prominent notch between the North and Central Towers on the mountain's northwest side. Above the slabs a system of cracks and

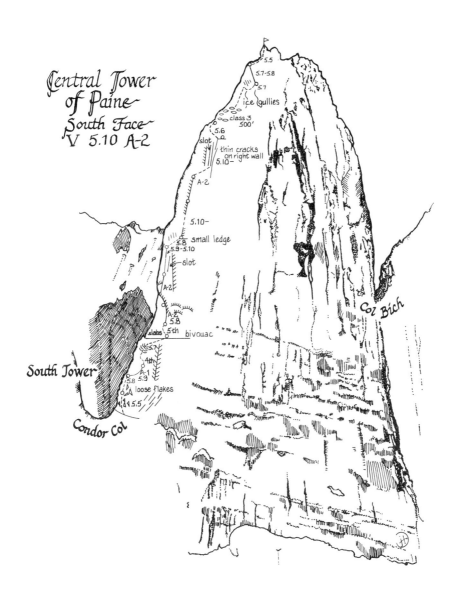

Central Tower
of Paine
South Face
V 5.10 A-2

5.5
5.7-5.8
5.7
ice gullies
class 3
500'
5.6
slot
thin cracks
on right wall
5.10-
A-2

5.10-
5.8 small ledge
5.9-5.10
slot
A-2
A-2
5.8
slabs 5th bivouac
5.7
4th
A-1
5.8 5.9
loose flakes
5.5

Col Bich

South Tower

Condor Col

dihedrals led to a gendarmed ridge below the summit. Not wasting any time, the climbers anchored ropes to the slabs to ensure safe passage up and down in foul weather and began pushing the route above Col Bich. Three hundred meters of vertical rock rose beyond the Col but after a month the British had gained only 24 meters on this difficult terrain. High winds, snow and cold temperatures inhibited progress and the climbers cursed the fact that they had missed the fine weather that had prevailed in October.

Below the Tower, the violent wind flattened their cloth mountain tents as if they were made of paper. The climbers tried to seal off the underside of a huge boulder with rocks to keep out the wind but dust and grit began to permeate everything, even the food they ate. During one of the nights that Bonington and Streetly spent under the boulder, a small stream of snow meltwater saturated the dry ground under Bonington's sleeping bag. As the temperature increased, the stream swelled and created a pool under the rock shelter. Not being in the mood for swimming, the sleepy pair evacuated their high camp.

As Christmas drew near, the expedition suspended work on the Tower and scuttled down to the estancia. A party atmosphere prevailed and, since the weather remained terrible, the British drank the available spirits. Days dragged on, the wind continued to hammer the mountain and morale plummeted. For the bedraggled British climbers, motivation came with the arrival of an Italian expedition, also keen on climbing the Central Tower. The Italian Alpine Club had carefully selected its older professional climbers to attempt the climb. The newcomers scowled at the heap of beer bottles outside the British tents and felt the ragtag crew of younger climbers had no business on "their" mountain. The Italians had not expected another climbing expedition to be in the area in the 1962-63 season; unfortunately, the Chilean government had allowed both groups on the same mountain.

A parley at dinner with the "Pope's mates", as Whillans referred to them, proved fruitless. The only common languages were bits of French and Spanish and the Italian's cool attitudes did not help toward an understanding of each party's position. An undeclared state of high pressure competition existed between the two teams; a "capture the flag" game was underway.

The Italians agreed not to utilize the line of British ropes already established on the mountain but to no more. In a hushed conference, the British formulated a plan to deal with the bad weather and maintain an advantage over their rivals. Bray and Whillans suggested they prefabricate a solid hut of wood and tarpaulin at the estancia, number the parts for easy reassembly and move it piece by piece up to the Tower. Thus the prototype of modern expedition box tents first came into being in Patagonia. The infant design lacked the clean lines and lightweight portability of later boxes but it did the job. Weighing 113 kilos, and with many of the timbers two meters long, it was not easy to transport. Discussion of the new device was kept quiet and the stack of "high tech" components was covered and guarded at all times.

The British chose New Year's Day to move the cumbersome box parts, in the hope that the Italians would be sleeping off hangovers. Once the British had established their hut near the foot of the Tower, two climbers remained in a good position to reach the mountain quickly and start climbing if the weather cleared. The Italians moved further up the slope and proudly erected their mountain tents among the boulders during a calm spell. The British watched and waited from the comfort of their 113 kilo, 2 x 2 x 1½ meter fort. Italian and Chilean flags gave the upper camp an official appearance. The British felt they too needed an ensign to represent their outpost and strung up a sad pair of long johns. When news of this unsightly gesture reached the British Embassy in Punta Arenas, authentic British and Chilean flags were quickly delivered.

During the next week Clough and Whillans snatched a day of calm weather and fixed line for several leads above the previous high point. The pair negotiated the rock pedestal, a shaft of granite that leans against the Tower, and a delicate traverse across a slab to the bottom of the Grey Dièdre, a prominent dihedral half way up the route. Here they stopped at the end of a hard day with an advancing storm in sight. Another week crept by and the climbers made no progress above the highest ropes. On the evening of 15 January with Bonington, Page, Streetly and Whillans at the hut, the sky cleared. At 4 the next morning, Bonington and Whillans started up, followed by Page and Streetly bringing bivouac gear and food. Quietly they tiptoed past the disheveled Italian camp. Tents sagged beneath broken poles, the proud flags were faded and tattered. Unaware of the fine day that had dawned, their opponents snored loudly.

Sunshine warmed the air, not a breath of wind disturbed the scene. Bonington and Whillans moved quickly up the fixed hemp ropes hand over hand, as they had no mechanical ascenders and chose not to prusik the ropes with slings. As Whillans started across the slab, the rope snapped above him. His feet held on the smooth slab as he inched his fingers toward the wind frayed broken end and tied it back to the one in his other hand.

After the tense moment with the broken rope, Bonington and Whillans began work on the Grey Dièdre, a smooth groove of grey rock and overhangs. Bonington climbed using direct aid; hammering in pitons to support his weight. He took a three meter fall when a piton pulled out but managed to reach a point where the climbing eased. Whillans took over the lead. Totally engrossed in the climbing, the lead pair did not notice the unusual drama taking place below.

When the Italians realized the wind had dropped, they peered from their tents and saw that the artful British had already climbed a considerable way up the Tower. Alarmed that their competitors might reach the summit first, they dressed hastily, grabbed some pitons and scrambled towards the Tower. Disregarding their previous promise not to use the British ropes, the Italians started up them. Page and Streetly, below Bonington and Whillans, brought up the rear guard. Furious that the five Italians were swarming upwards, Page and Streetly began to pull the fixed ropes up out of reach. Undaunted by this tactic, the Italians continued to climb. The comic scene finally ended when Page and Streetly could climb no higher and stopped pulling up rope behind them. They turned back but shouted a warning to Bonington and Whillans about the Italian threat.

Whillans led up the Red Dièdre, a square cut corner of reddish brown granite, placing pitons sparingly. By 5 pm the two climbers had reached the shoulder, from where the route to the summit wound around and over gendarmes of rock, some of them coated with a layer of verglas and snow. Bonington and Whillans spent two-and-a-half hours on the tricky ridge and reached the top of the 2460 meter peak at 7:30 pm on 16 January 1963. The evening remained windless and they shouted news of their victory to the other climbers six hundred meters below. They wondered if the Italians could hear them too; not that it mattered any more. As the light faded, the tired pair banged in a piton to mark the summit and descended one hundred meters to the shoulder, where they bivouaced for the night.

In the morning Bonington and Whillans began to rappel and encountered the Italians on their way up. Bonington described the meeting that took place.
"First there is Aste and Aiazzi. They glower at us, but then on the next ledge, is big friendly Taldo. He grins happily, shakes hands and says in broken English, "It is good you getting to the top. This is your route. We should not be here." Taldo and his companions gained the summit at 5 pm on 17 January, twenty hours after the first ascent.

The "Whillan's Box" which was so instrumental in the ascent of the Central Tower, remained intact as late as 1983 when it was utilized by a Chilean expedition. By 1991 the little hut had lost its fabric to the winds, exposing a bleached and twisted wooden framework, an artifact from a great climb.

First ascent of the South Tower: 1963

When Italians Armando Aste, Josve Aiazzi, Carluccio Casati, Nando Nusdeo and Vasco Taldo learned the British planned to attack the smooth and imposing Southwest Ridge of the South Tower, they mobilized for an attempt on the North Ridge. At the end of January the five climbers prepared the first 180 meters of vertical, grey granite with fixed ropes and retreated to a high camp to wait for good weather. On 8 February Aste and Taldo started up the ropes after hearing the British were within one day of the summit. The Italians were already despondent about the British beating them to the summit of the Central Tower and Taldo voiced his opinion about the situation. "When you're unlucky, you're unlucky from the beginning to the end." Aiazzi, Casati and Nusdeo formed a second team and followed several hours behind.

The two lead climbers gained their previous high point and loaded up with pitons and canned food for the summit. Aste took the lead and climbed up to a vertical crack and then a grey dihedral. Still employing direct aid, he pounded shaky pitons behind flakes and large loose blocks to a point where the rock imroved and a crack led to the shoulder. The climbing had been tedious and the pair ran out of daylight as they neared a ledge. Although surrounded by rotten rock, the two climbers sat on their rope for insulation and opened a can of chicken and two beers for dinner.

In the morning they climbed two more pitches before the angle eased and they reached the shoulder at the base of the final slender ridge. Here the pair dumped unnecessary gear and took only twenty pitons, a bolt kit, camera, Italian flag and fluid. The rock changed and Aste and Taldo climbed on the superb orange-yellow granite that has made the Towers famous. The climbing was primarily free and, with lighter packs, the two Italians moved fast, gaining the summit at 3 pm. They found no evidence of previous climbers and celebrated their victory over the British with a sip of whiskey and tomato juice. The Italians learned later that the opposition had reached within three hundred meters of the top on the Southwest Ridge. Aste and Taldo left behind an ice piton graced with a red, white and blue ribbon as the invisible wind began to blow from the west.

The summit pair descended and met Aiazzi, Casati and Nusdeo still climbing toward the top, which they reached late in the day. All five bivouaced a second night near the shoulder as the storm worsened. On 10 February the wind was so fierce on the descent that the climbers lowered the first man down to anchor the rappel ropes and keep them from blowing out of their grasp. Below the bivouac a rock hit Taldo, smashing in the side of his helmet and injuring his shoulder and hip. He remained conscious and with help reached the bottom of the Tower safely.

Even with an injured member, the climbers cleaned the fixed ropes off the mountain and removed their high camp. In twenty-one pitches of climbing the Italians had completed a remarkable ascent that would not be repeated for two decades.

First ascent of the Fortress: 1968

With the ascents of the three Towers, subsequent expeditions began to look for new challenges in the Paine group. Nearly a dozen peaks remained that offered difficult climbing by their easiest routes. A few kilometers to the west of the Towers, there rose the most massive unclimbed granite mountain of the range, the Fortress. This 2700 meter peak is situated between the head of the Río Ascencio and Río Francés Valleys and comprises perpendicular walls from 900 to 1500 meters high. The summit of black slate is capped by a long ridge of bizarre rime and snow mushrooms.

In 1966 Derek Walter, a British schoolteacher in Punta Arenas, made two reconnaissance trips to study the mountain's weaknesses, as a British group planned to attempt the peak a year later and needed information about routes and approaches. Walter concluded that one side was not as sheer as the others and that an approach up the Francés Valley to attempt the west face would be best. A band of seven climbers from Britain and two from Chile installed an advance base camp among gnarled beech trees in the upper Río Francés Valley by December 1967. Ropes, food and tentage had to be transported up the valley to just below the mountain. Dave Nicol and John Gregory went ahead of the others to the slopes of the Fortress to investigate the terrain. The two scouts looked for suitable sites to erect box tents and establish camps on the mountain.

The Whillans' box had undergone modifications since it was first put to use on the Central Tower as a means of coping with the high winds. Manufactured in Britain from bolted angle iron covered with a tightly stretched skin of canvas, the box was storm proof and weighed about eighteen kilos. Lighter weight materials also made the whole thing much more portable. Ropes were of nylon or perlon, not hemp, and mechanical ascenders, which were safer than grabbing the ropes with bare hands, maintained a tight grip on fixed ropes. Free climbing and direct aid climbing techniques had improved, so increasingly difficult pitches could be ascended more quickly. Siege climbing remained the prevalent mode of attacking the mountain; it would be eight more years before a climbing party severed themselves from the umbilical cord of fixed ropes and camps on a major technical face in the Paine.

During the first month on the Fortress, the climbers struggled up a long snow couloir of moderate steepness, anchoring box tents, of which they had brought several, at the top and bottom. Above the gully rose ninety meters of steep ice that filled a narrow constriction they named the Ice Hose. One hundred meters of steep snow and a short difficult rock pitch brought them to the Terrace and location of their highest and final camp where Ian Clough, Gordon Hibberd and Chris Jackson erected a tent.

For almost three hundred meters the climbers ascended difficult rock in the Big Corner, a feature visible from the valley. Gregory and Jackson front pointed up a sixty degree ice bulge and made a startling discovery at the top. An old red Perlon rope lay buried in the ice and on a rock ledge, to the side of the couloir, lay a pile of pitons and wooden wedges. This evidence worried them and they wondered if a previous party had already climbed the Fortress. Apprehensively, Gregory and Jackson continued on up the Big Corner but, to their relief, found no further sign of the mystery climbers. When the expedition returned home they learned more about the hardware unearthed high on the Fortress. Several years earlier, Italians Armando Aste and Franco Solina had attempted the mountain from the Río Ascencio Valley to the northeast. The two climbers climbed to a col between the Fortress and the Shield, probably to scale the Northeast Ridge of the Fortress but found it too difficult. A ledge system on the west face must have drawn them to the base of the Big Corner, up which they climbed part way. The legend is that the Italians spent nine consecutive bivouacs on the mountain. According to Clough,

"In view of the instability of Patagonian weather, this attempt could be regarded as quite bold."

For the British climbers on the mountain, the hard work was not over. The last 120 meters to the gentle summit slopes consisted of overhanging loose rock that demanded direct aid and caution. Occasional rays of warm sun melted ice and dislodged rocks. A final steep crack took four hours to lead and ended on a 1.6 kilometer long gradual slope below the summit. Because of the wind, Hibberd, the leader, could not communicate with Gregory and Nicol below. His haul line had snagged and the two belayers grew frustrated trying to free it. All three descended to the Terrace, then down to advance base camp where they recuperated for their summit attempt the following day.

Once up the fixed ropes the next morning, the trio scrambled along scree slopes for a kilometer to steeper ground on the north side of a ridge of ice mushrooms. As they traversed, each mushroom ahead appeared to be the summit but further away was always another higher blob of ice. Eventually they gained a col below the final nine meter high mushroom, bridged up a steep chimney and, amid swirling clouds, stood on the summit. The clouds parted to reveal the Shield, the three Towers and a dark storm approaching from the ice cap. For a moment the summit was theirs. Far below, the six other expedition members watched through binoculars with glee as Hibberd, Gregory and Nicol stood on top.

First ascent of Cuerno Principal: 1968

Shortly after the first ascent of the Fortress, Ian Clough led a British attempt on 2100m Cuerno Principal. The British retreated after Nikki Clough broke her ankle. Helping with the evacuation were Chilean university students Raul Aguilera, Eduardo García, Osvaldo Latorre and Gastón Oyarzún. These four Chilean climbers then spent two days completing the first ascent of the peak on 31 January by its north and west side. The final ninety meter tower of black slate provided the hardest climbing. Of the forty days the Chileans spent in the area, only four were good enough for climbing. There were some who had doubts as to whether the Chilean climbers had reached the summit. In 1976 Jack Miller, a veteran of several rafting and exploratory expeditions to Patagonia, and his party found conclusive evidence on top during the second ascent of the peak. The Chileans had left a paper plate with their names and date of ascent and had dedicated the mountain to their girlfriends and mothers. This was their proof.

First ascent of Catedrál: 1971

Two veterans of the Fortress climb, Chris Jackson and Dave Nicol, joined with British climbers Guy Lee, Bob Shaw, Bob Smith and Roger Whewell for an attempt on the austere Catedrál. This 2200 meter peak is situated at the head of the Francés Valley, five kilometers northeast of the Grey Glacier. The west side of the peak rises above the large Perro Glacier, which fills the valley between the peaks on the east side of the Francés Valley and the Olguin Range (Cerro Olguin and Cerro Ostrava) which borders the ice cap. Worse than normal weather prevailed; the day they chose to attempt the west ridge of the unexplored peak it remained calm only until afternoon. In a month and a half this was the climbers' only opportunity to try the ridge. The spine of rock stretched for 21 rope lengths; the climbing entailed both traversing the smooth sides of huge gendarmes and straddling narrow sections. The six climbers fixed two lengths of rope, but their ascent was primarily an alpine style dash to reach the top before the oncoming storm.

On the first rappel off the summit their rope jammed; the frantic climbers began climbing down the ridge rather than attemptting to free the rope. The situation became desperate as the wind blowing from across the ice cap strengthened. Nicol found the descent taxed his supply of adrenalin. "On the crest of the ridge proper the gusts were terrifying; at times one actually had to pull oneself down the roped arete. On the Northeast Ridge large pieces of sun loosened ice broke off and, unbelievably, flew upwards to disappear into the maelstrom of the mountain's eddy."

East Face of the Central Tower: 1974

The Catedrál ascent showed that to climb alpine style in Patagonia a group had to be decisive and move rapidly. Mistakes were out of the question and climbers limited themselves to the shorter routes. The giant, untouched vertical faces remained intimidating. It was enough just to attempt a big wall; most parties preferred the security of fixed ropes.

It was not until 1971 that the Central Tower's East Face first felt the blow of a piton hammer; when a group of South Africans ascended the needle like Sword and precipitous, black capped Cuerno Norte. With time and supplies left over, they made an attempt on the Central Tower's large East Face. For twelve hundred meters the sheer cliff looms above the Torre Glacier that gnaws at the Tower's base. In the upper half a prominent dihedral drops from the summit ridge as though a line had been traced by a falling rock. The dihedral was a natural choice for the South Africans; they climbed one-third of the route before storms and diminishing supplies forced a retreat.

In 1974 South Africans Paul Fatti, Roger Fuggle, Art McGarr, Mervyn Prior, Mike Scott and Richard Smithers returned with the East Face as their primary objective. Paul Fatti, their leader, had climbed extensively in the Alps, as well as making the third ascent of the difficult Troll Wall in Norway. He had also put up a number of new routes on the Blowberg near his home in Johannesberg. Roger Fuggle had made the second pitonless ascent of El Capitan's Nose in Yosemite, and had nearly reached the summit of Fitz Roy by the Supercouloir the year before. Collectively, the group had a wide range of climbing experience that included ice and rock in the Alps, South Africa, Yosemite and Patagonia.

Box tents had continued to be refined; by the early 1970's a coated nylon skin enveloped a collapsible framework of aluminum. The expedition purchased a seven kilo *Karrimor Box* in Britain for $140, confident it would be easier to transport. Shortly after the climbers had secured a new box below the Tower, a heavy snowfall nearly crushed it with the occupants inside. Perhaps the 113 kilo dinosaur of eleven years earlier would have performed better. Fuggle and Prior moved to a snug snow cave just before Christmas and looked outside to see their box uprooted from its anchors by a wind gust and blown out of sight.

For thirty-two days the six climbers hammered pitons and slotted nuts into cracks on the vertical rock. They had brought along two of the early Lowe camming nuts and found them very useful in cracks seven to fifteen centimeters wide. Intricate direct aid climbing consumed most of their effort; they spent a large amount of time rappelling the face and reascending fixed ropes. Art McGarr

105

referred to the climb as a "gigantic construction project." Pitons had to be driven behind fragile billboard size wafers of granite, with pendulums negotiated at the end of a rope to reach other crack systems. The cold weather and spindrift avalanches caused by heavy snowfalls made the strenuous climbing just that much more difficult. Fixed ropes decorated the entire face; the freezing and thawing conditions created some unusual problems. Scott found reascending the ropes after a storm to be a nerve wracking operation. "Ice as thick as our arms surrounded some sections of the rope; we spent hours at scraping the cold rope and skidding alarmingly down until the jumar teeth finally bit in."

Fatti and Prior finally gained the summit ridge to be confronted by the maze of drunken towers that had slowed down Bonington and Whillans in 1963. Barely enough light remained for their descent. Frustrated, the pair started down. Just above the East Face, Prior took a 22 meter fall when an anchor pulled out as he changed from one fixed rope to another. Although unconscious at first, he came to and, with the help of Fuggle, McGarr and Fatti, descended the wall at night by the light of headlamps. From below, their lights twinkled on the dark Tower in a slow downward procession that lasted for twenty-one hours, well into the following day. With broken ribs and an impacted vertebra, Prior walked on down to base camp. At the estancia he got a ride to the hospital in Puerto Natales. While he recuperated, the weather flexed its muscles and plastered the face with ice and snow for nine consecutive days. Scott and Smithers stayed in the humid snow cave and waited.

On 20 January the barometer began to rise as the two damp and bedsore climbers started up the twelve hundred meters of fixed rope. Iced ropes slowed their progress and Scott and Smithers only managed to reach a makeshift bivouac site. Scott told of how the evening passed. "Snow was falling as we tried to heat water, then the clouds unzipped and started waves of snow down the dihedral. Richard piled into his hammock but I was too late. Snow was crashing down so heavily that I couldn't empty a load of snow from mine before it was filled again. Finally I jumped in, boots and all, no hope of getting into a sleeping bag, and shivered through the night." The next day, two months after they had begun their climb, the pair scrambled up the final tower, which rises but a few meters higher than the surrounding spikes of rock. They recognized peaks 160 kilometers away; nearby the South Tower and Fortress pierced the sky with their clean lines.

It is unfortunate that these pristine mountains are so often marred by man's passage. The South Africans, like other expeditions that siege a route, left a number of ropes hanging from the wall. Their way of rationalizing this apathy towards the removal of all the rope was one commonly used in Patagonia, and elsewhere.

"The wind would soon dispose of the nylon spaghetti," wrote Scott. That is not necessarily the case; Jim Donini found scraps of rope on Cerro Torre 17 years after Maestri and Egger had been there. The value of the equipment is a big factor; Art McGarr said, "This industrial grade nylon hardly cost us anything so we had no intention of reusing it." It is not enough to climb a mountain by a demanding route. Even greater effort is required to leave the mountain close to the state in which it was discovered.

First ascent of the Mummer: 1976

Techniques and technology advanced, along with a bolder attitude toward climbing. Mental barriers that had inhibited "impossible" ascents in the Fitz Roy and Torre region began to disintegrate. Nevertheless, whether alpine style ascents of larger faces would catch on in the Paine was uncertain. Already two separate failures by the British and New Zealanders on the steeple like Mummer indicated that this unconventional approach was doomed. Every side of this attractive 1850 meter peak offered smooth and nearly vertical walls for over 600 meters, with one face exceeding 900 meters.

On the mountain's Southwest Face, two South African climbers made a daring attempt to reach the summit in a single push, relying only on one hundred meters of fixed rope in tricky spots. This was a departure from the hundreds of meters of fixed rope previously used on major walls; and would be much easier to clean later. To succeed they had to keep the size of their party very small, climb rapidly and possess the perseverance to reascend the mountain after each storm forced them to retreat. Without much fixed rope, the duo had to reclimb most of the difficult rock pitches, a tedious job. On larger expeditions someone else can take up the slack when a climber gets tired or loses motivation. In a team of two, all of the responsibility and physical hardship falls on only four shoulders.

However, the two South Africans were a hardy pair. Inside the snow cave, below where the steep climbing began, Dave Cheesemond and Phil Dawson played chess and cards to pass the stormy days. At age 24, Cheesemond was already a veteran of serious alpine climbs and big walls throughout the world. (In the ensuing eleven years he climbed many extreme alpine routes in North America, a number of them first ascents; he was killed during an attempt on the Hummingbird Ridge of Mount Logan in 1987.)

On the Mummer the two South Africans remained snug in their cave and, through the tunnel entrance, kept a constant watch on the weather conditions. The change occurred swiftly, one morning not a hint of wind or patch of clouds blemished the sky. They started up immediately; in two days of climbing they covered twenty pitches of difficult rock, mostly free with some direct aid. One uncomfortable bivouac on the first night passed quickly as the summer night was only six hours long at the 52 degree southern latitude. Cheesemond and Dawson made it to the summit late on the second day after a delicate climb up snow covered rock. It was 7 December and they stood on top for only five minutes before descending into a thickening storm. But at least they had achieved their goal: many who come to Patagonia do not.

Southeast Face of the Fortress: 1979 attempt

Three years after the first ascent of the Mummer, an even more ambitious group arrived in the Paine. The objective of British climbers Phil Burke, Mick Horlov and Keith Myhill was the unclimbed 1650 meter Southeast Face of the Fortress. They chose to live on the wall and had designed a "super box" of heavy duty *Gore-Tex* and *Cordura*, with a carbon fiber frame that could be suspended from the rock without a ledge. The box had changed radically in sixteen years. It had dropped in weight from a knee buckling 113 kilos to six kilos, with petrochemical fabrics and frames replacing canvas and wood. The two boxes were worlds apart in design and materials but less than three kilometers apart in distance. The original "Hotel Britannico" still sat below the Central Tower where it was erected in 1963. High on the Fortress, Burke, Horlov and Myhill were glad to have a compact and reliable shelter with them on the wall, as protection against the wind and almost constant snowfall. Even so, they had problems with the wind, as Burke pointed out. "Given a severe Patagonian storm you will disappear like a giant box kite; eventually the doors blew in due to the zippers shattering."

The three climbers fixed rope above their bivouac sites, moved up and then repeated the process. Eight of the forty pitches were artificial, and the free climbing was consistently difficult. On their third attempt to gain the summit they did not return to the comfort of flat ground for thirteen days. The climbers opted to retreat in a frightful storm at a point one rope length below the terrace of black slate that leads to the summit. The Southeast Face had been protected from the fierce winds but not so the terraced slopes above. Burke's hands froze and the disappointed climbers could only descend without making the summit.

This climb showed that a bold approach, highly skilled personnel and special gear were possibly the means to scaling other great faces in the Paine group. Patagonia has proven repeatedly that climbers must possess qualities beyond technical skill and fitness. The "sky blue" Paine mountains rarely appear blue and usually they are engulfed by wind or precipitation. Only if a window of settled weather presents itself can determined climbers have a chance to make an alpine ascent and grab a summit.

East Face of Paine Grande: 1984

The great East Face of Paine Grande rises 2133 meters from the glacier at its base and is a distinctly different type of climb from anything else in the Paine. It is not a granite wall but rather several hanging glaciers smeared on rotten sedimentary rock perched at precarious angles. Avalanches sweep the face regularly in the form of slabs, spindrift sloughs and ice séracs. In short, the East Face of the mountain is very dangerous.

Three South African climbers arrived in the Parque Nacional Torres del Paine in November of 1984 to attempt the unclimbed South Face of the Fortress. John Davies, Hilton Davies and Chris Lomax decided to attempt Paine Grande after a month of bad weather and excessive rockfall on the Fortress. Of the three, only Lomax had been to the Paine before, when he tried the Fortress in 1978 with Dave Cheesemond.

On 4 December the climbers left their base camp in the upper Francés Valley for an alpine style ascent of Paine Grande. They carried food and stove fuel for six days, and a snow shovel for digging ledges and caves for sleeping. Once across the Francés River and the crevassed glacier leading to the East Face, they paused to watch an avalanche run its course before starting their ascent. A rock ridge enabled the trio to climb unroped for 170 meters, until the difficulties demanded a belay. Three pitches of rock climbing ended below a huge boulder, where the South Africans flattened the snow and spent the night.

For most of the second day the climbers followed a couloir of snow and ice while avalanches rumbled down the face on either side. Near the top of the couloir, Hilton's crampon fell off. Hardly had he refastened it when Chris lost his grip on the ice and fell 52 meters, to be held by John's belay. As they emerged from the gully it was scoured by icefall. The tired alpinists struggled to climb hard, brittle ice on a vertical wall as the evening temperature dropped to -20C. They hoped the morning sun would soften the ice and make the pitch easier.

The third day was hot and warm. Chris quickly led the ice wall; then hauled up their packs. Thus far they had experienced good weather, but with it the warmth that loosens snow and ice. During the day an ice wall gave way; later a large snow and ice avalanche obliterated their fresh tracks below. Under these circumstances, John, Hilton and Chris chose to continue climbing on through the night when conditions were cold and stable. It was as though an invisible hand were erasing their route behind them. They could not turn back; their only chance was to make the summit and then descend the safer and shorter Southwest Face.

On the fourth day a storm hit the mountain with wind and driving snow. Just when they most needed visibility, it was replaced by piercing ice in their faces and swirling spindrift. The climbers bivouaced below the final rock wall and suffered frostbite from dehydration and the cold. They climbed up into the storm and fierce wind the next day until they found a suitable site for a snow cave, where they dug in.

For two more days the climbers tried to find the descent route down the southwest side in the storm. At one point an entire ice wall gave way just below them as they were arguing whether to descend that route. The exhausted group searched elsewhere. With food and fuel expended, they finally found the route down on the eighth day; a series of gullies that led below the clouds and out of danger.

The ascent of the East Face was a remarkable climb, fraught with danger every step of the way. An outside observer might consider the route to be suicidal, What one person considers risky, another may not. The route may never receive a second ascent, but it was a climb that was cleverly executed in impeccable style, without using a scrap of fixed rope. With "sport alpinism" beginning to infiltrate the mountains it might be wise to pay closer attention to the "means" of an ascent; not just the "ends".

7

THE CENTRAL TOWER'S SOUTH FACE - 1981

"Do you feel lucky?", I asked Bobby Knight in the autumn of 1980. "Yeah, sure", he replied cheerfully. "Good, then let's do an expedition to the Towers of Paine next year." With Bobby's light-hearted consent, I had found a partner for my first climbing adventure in Patagonia. Our objective would be a new route up the nine hundred meter South Face of the Central Tower, using minimal fixed rope and no support from other climbers (see Appendix III).

Throughout the next twelve months I dug through journals and magazines to learn what routes had been climbed in the Paine and to get a feel for what the environment would be like. Few climbers had visited this small range of granite spires; those I interviewed had strong opinions, both positive and negative.

"The Paine is a fantastic area! There are new routes to be done everywhere you look and the rock is incredibly solid," Dave Cheesemond had told me, when our paths crossed in Yosemite in 1981. He traipsed around the valley in a ratty pair of mud spattered long-johns; plucking at his beard in the rain. Although dour at first, his face immediately brightened at the mention of Patagonia; we spent an entire afternoon gabbing about possible routes, what food was available and the type of equipment to bring along. Cheesemond's news was good.

Don Peterson had made an attempt on Cerro Torre to the north; his remarks revealed the other side of climbing in Patagonia. "It's a terrible place, just terrible. The wind blows constantly; when it stops and the sun comes out, the snow and rime ice melts causing streams to pour down the walls. Rain gear is useless. It's just awful."

After talking with Peterson, Bobby was ready to call off the trip. I threw my hands in the air and waved them frantically. "Don't listen to Peterson. He had a rotten time down there. We'll have a great trip. Come on, let's go." Bobby threw me a doubtful glance but finally yielded to my cajoling. The discussion changed from "Are we going?" to "What gear are we taking?".

We had to select our equipment carefully, as the airlines charged fifty dollars for each excess piece of baggage. A lot of hardware was needed, not only to climb the South Face of the Central Tower but also to rappel back down it. Seventeen to twenty fifty meter rappels would consume thirty-four to forty anchors, assuming we placed two anchors at each stance. We chose three dozen steel and aluminum pitons, from dime thick knife blades to ten centimeter wide bongs. For cracks not clogged with ice and snow, thirty aluminum stoppers and hex nuts would work nicely; we packed these in nylon duffels along with eight *Friends.*

Our taped boxes and duffels began to bulge at the seams as we stuffed in ninety meters of nylon webbing, two fifty meter 11mm Perlon lead ropes, two fifty meter 8mm haul lines, fifty aluminum carabiners, four ice tools, rigid crampons, rock shoes and leather double boots. Polypropylene underwear, pile jackets and pants, a neoprene windsurfing jacket, neoprene socks, waterproof outer garments, synthetic sleeping bags weighing 1.4 kilos and a one kilo *Gore-Tex* bivouac tent filled the left over spaces.

With the addition of camping gear, cook pots and food for forty days, the packing was finished. There were still last minute errands to accomplish before leaving on a two month expedition to a foreign country. In the frantic final days of organizing our trip, I found little time to reflect upon my motivation for going to Patagonia. As I settled into the dentist's soft reclining chair, he asked me where I was going climbing. "To Patagonia where the wind is terrifying and rime ice plasters the mountains; where if you climb for two days in every month you are lucky." There was a long silence, then he asked, "So, why are you going? It sounds horrible." My response was not very convincing. "Well, the mountains are beautiful and there are a lot of unclimbed granite faces." My dentist frowned and got to work.

----

17. Cuernos Principal, Cuernos Oriental and Lake Pehoe from the south. The first ascent of Cuernos Principal in 1968 by the Chileans went up the North Face, hidden in this view. *Nikon F3, 105mm lens, Fujichrome Velvia*

18. The Central and North Paine Towers and the Black Nest of the Condors from the southeast. Author's 1982 route followed the left skyline of the Central Tower. The 1974 South African route is just left of the right skyline, while the 1963 first ascent route is on the right side. The Italians climbed the North Tower in 1958 by the left-hand ridge. *Nikon F3, 105mm lens, Fujichrome*

19. The North and Central Paine Towers from the west. The first ascent of the North Tower by the Italians followed the right-hand ridge. The British first ascent route of the Central Tower was up the left side; Americans climbed a new route up the right skyline in 1982. *Nikon F3, 50mm lens, Fujichrome*

20. Hanging camp on the East Buttress of the Fortress. Author's 1990-91 team was turned back less than halfway up the 1979 route due to bad weather and loose rock. *Nikon FM2, 16mm lens, Fujichrome*

What I didn't tell him was that I had wanted to visit Patagonia ever since I had begun climbing seriously, some twelve years earlier. Photographs in journals and magazines enticed me; I was certain this was one dream I must fulfill. The whirring drill bit deeper into my tooth but the novocaine and soft background music transported me south to a wild land of icy peaks.

Seven days after leaving Oregon I got my first view of the Towers of Paine. Tearing along the gravel roads of the Pampas at eighty kilometers an hour in a rental car, I spotted the mountains from a distance of thirty-two kilometers. The 2400 meter summits jutted from the foothills at the edge of the grass and scrub covered plains. Brown granite walls rose nine hundred to fifteen meters on every side, while a thick layer of grey clouds moved rapidly across the sky. I could feel the wind buffetting the car, hurling pieces of gravel at its sides. Without question, the wind would be far worse on the face of the Central Tower which we were intending to climb.

We unloaded our two hundred kilos of gear and food at Estancia Radic and bargained with the gauchos for horses. From the Estancia it was eight kilometers to our proposed base camp in the Río

---

21. Approaching the East Buttress of The Fortress. In 1979 a British team climbed from the toe of the Buttress to within one pitch of the easier slopes leading to the summit. In 1989 the Italians climbed the right skyline. In 1990 a Yugoslav team completed a new route just right of the Buttress using a thousand meters of fixed rope. *Nikon F3, 24mm lens, Fujichrome*

22. The East Face of Paine Grande as viewed from the summit of the Central Tower of Paine. The South Africans climbed the Face in 1984; Italians made the first ascent of the mountain from the opposite side in 1957. *Nikon FM, 24mm lens, Kodachrome 64*

23. Bobby Knight reluctantly preparing to reascend our wind-frayed ropes on the third of four attempts on the South Face of the Central Tower of Paine. *Nikon FM, 24mm lens, K 64*

24. North Ridge of the South Tower of Paine from the Central Tower. The 1963 first ascent route went from the lower right, up onto the low angle slab, then directly up the North Ridge. *Nikon FM, 24mm lens, K 64*

Ascencio Valley; we didn't relish making four trips apiece when we could spend $25 on horses. The haggling went on as I paid a visit to the outhouse in back. A violent gust of wind found a hole low on one side of the tilted shack, blowing urine up into my face. I thought it was humorous at the time; that was early in the trip.

My energy was overflowing, the sky had cleared and the wind dropped to a gentle breeze as we made our way up the beech choked valley toward base camp. We chose to camp at the site established by the South Africans in 1971 and 1974. The only signs that anyone had camped there were an old fire ring, a crude table of tree limbs and tin can lids with names inscribed on them. Even though the place smelled of damp leaves and rotting wood, it gave us the feeling of a makeshift home. Above our camp the towers gleamed against a blue sky; I was positive we could pick off our climb quickly. The many accounts written by climbers in the Paine, of weeks of wind, rain, snow and repeated failures, seemed like fiction. I said to Bobby, "Let's take up a couple days of food and climb the Tower." But we ended up taking far more than food; hardware, extra rope, sleeping bags and our bivouac tent. We approached the mountain as though the weather would remain good and we could bivouac comfortably. Patagonia was about to teach us a lesson!

The weather started to change on the first evening, as we made a carry up to the base of the mountain. A dull roar emanated from the col between the South and Central towers, followed closely by cloud streamers trailing off the summits. Maybe the stories were true. "This is just a little storm." I was right. The wind blew, snow fell on the mountain and it rained in the beech forest for only five days. Bobby decided to carry more gear and food up to the edge of the glacier and stash it under a huge boulder while I repaired clothing at basecamp. He was almost at the boulder with a twenty-two kilo load when a powerful gust of wind knocked him flat. Nothing was broken but I sensed his cheerful spirit had received a blow.

Feeling the need to have some kind of camp close to the mountain, we ascended the gentle glacier to a suitable site for a snow cave. The slope below the South Tower was two hundred meters from a moderate gully of ice and snow leading to the South Face of the Central Tower. This seemed like a good spot for us to dig a burrow that would shelter us from the elements. Only the large craters made by falling rocks caused us to worry, but there seemed to be no alternative.

I have always disliked digging and living in snow caves. Clothing and sleeping bags remain damp, ceilings sag in warm temperatures and the dark, icy walls are depressing. Knowing my loathing for the task, Bobby began digging, furiously hurling chunks of snow down the slope. I tidied up our veranda; creating more space for the human steam shovel to work. Every few minutes I would interject encouraging comments to spur him on. "Good work. What a nice shape the doorway has. Gosh, you're almost finished. Want me to lend a hand?"

A few projections hung down from the low ceiling; our 1½ × 2 meter floor needed some leveling out. The warm glow of a candle softened the icy appearance as, like trap door spiders, we pulled everything in and sealed the entrance as best we could. There is one great advantage to cave dwelling; you cannot hear the storm outside. This feature allows sleep to come easily but it also prevents the inhabitants from detecting the end of a storm. In Patagonia this is critical; to utilize every hour of calm weather, one must begin climbing the minute a storm abates.

The very night we moved into our hole, the wind died to a whisper. Clouds that had blotted out the sky vanished; stars sparkled in the heavens. Without a chance to catch our breath, we would attempt the nine hundred meter South Face in the morning. Such was the nature of this capricious land. We had to be ready to move as soon as conditions changed, whether we wanted to or not. I did not want to. Just the sight of the face had turned my stomach into knots. An accident on this mountain would be the end of us. There were no other climbers nearby, nor anyone else who could help in an emergency. Every move we made must be carefully thought out; each piece of equipment scrutinized. I swallowed three antacid tablets and tried to sleep. At least we had brought along excellent bivouac gear and should be comfortable high on the face.

In the predawn hours we began preparing for the climb, to my dismay the sky was still clear and windless. We spent ten hours climbing, reaching a level spot just as the weather changed. The last two hundred meters was up steep granite comprised of loose flakes, vertical cracks and smooth slabs. My pack was a burden, as were the extra ropes we hauled up. I was exhausted. Already the wind speed had increased dramatically. Three-hundred- and-sixty meters separated us from the security of our snow cave on the glacier below.

Here on the ledge, the wind tore at our bivouac tent with frightening power. Confident about our one kilo shelter, we didn't hesitate to excavate a snow bank and anchor the guy lines to pitons. The thin layer of fabric which we had hoped would protect us from the storm was beginning to tear apart at the seams; the sound of the flapping tent had started to drive me mad. There was nothing to do but collapse the tent and burrow into what remained of the snow bank. The thought of descending in the dark made me retch, so with my ice hammer and fingers, I scraped out a hole sixty centimeters in diameter and one meter deep.

Bobby stretched out on the open ledge with his feet inside a pack, with the haul bag pulled up over his head. Within my snow coffin I squirmed and thrashed to get comfortable; outside the wind velocity continued to increase. This was one nightmare that refused go away, I was scared. In desperation, I wriggled out of my hole and tried to cover myself with the bivouac tent. The wind caught the tent like a parachute and started to drag me off the ledge. There were six meters of slack rope between my harness and the piton above. With the help of adrenalin, I stuffed the billowing tent at three times normal speed and clawed my way back into my tiny cave.

The night passed with agonizing slowness. As dawn approached we quickly organized ourselves and did three rappels to just above the col. At this point we were 54 meters above the snow but with only 50 meter rappel ropes. With reluctance I backed over the edge. Just above the snow, I ran out of rope and began pounding in a piton to anchor the bottom so that it wouldn't blow away. The wind, forced into a slot sixty meters wide between the South and Central towers, blew my body into a near horizontal position. All I could do to keep from being blown clear across the wall was to stop pounding and clutch desperately at a flake.

How safe it felt to be back inside our damp cave. Not a breath of wind stirred within its walls, the floor was smooth and we could soothe our parched throats with hot tea, cocoa and *Jell-O*. The day before our lives had been in peril. Even so, after one day's rest in the cave, I began to think of a second attempt on the route. In my journal I scribbled my hopes for going back up when the weather cleared. Our savage bivouac and descent had a severe effect on Bobby; he said, "If we don't make it this next time, I don't know if we will at all." I wrote in my journal, "Well, that's nonsense, but if he fizzles it'll be hard to convince him otherwise." Some thoughts are best unspoken; I did not want to sacrifice Bobby's friendship for my own ambition. Tactfully, I tried to prepare him for facing a third and even a fourth attempt on the tower.

During the next month our efforts at climbing the mountain developed a distinct pattern. From our beech forest base camp we checked the weather every morning at 2 am. If the sky was clear and no wind audible, we ate a quick breakfast of oatmeal; then hiked for five hours to the base of the route. Twice we climbed high on the face, only to have the wind return. Twice we retreated to base camp to nurse our battered bodies and hopes. The monotonous weeks passed slowly but, by making slight changes in the regular routine, our sanity remained relatively intact.

Base camp life consisted of eating, reading and sleeping. Cooking up a special dinner or making a batch of popcorn momentarily distracted our sullen thoughts. Unfortunately, our food supplies did not allow extravagant eating. I had planned the food back home, soliciting Bobby's suggestions and additions. He had little to say about it then, but later complained that the lack of snack food was hindering his enjoyment of the trip. "You didn't help me plan the food in Portland, so we're stuck with what we brought." I spat out the words like bullets; later that afternoon Bobby apologized.

I, too, was not without fault. Bobby's cooking habits were not like my meticulous ways. He was constantly burning the pudding to the pan bottom. Each time I nagged at him he became more disgusted with me. I could see the irritation within him about to burst, so I apologized. Like any successful relationship, ours demanded the willingness to admit mistakes and communicate feelings before they became problems. Our very lives depended on our ability to work together. The many weeks of waiting out storms and failures put our partnership to the ultimate test. Several times when the wind blew really hard in base camp, the ground rose and fell slightly as the tree roots pryed at the boulders beneath the surface. The stones rubbed against each with an unearthly growling sound, like a set of giant teeth grinding together. It didn't exactly lull us to sleep.

To break up the base camp routine, I would take short hikes through the woods; on one daring trip I was gone for two-and-a-half days to Lago Nordenskjöld. The nearby lake was a peaceful change from base camp; I enjoyed being alone. On a tiny fire, I brewed up coffee and settled back to a lazy morning of reading my Louis L'Amour Western. Wood smoke mingled with the smell of hot coffee; it almost made me forget the battering winds, frightening rappels and aching muscles and joints. The Tower seemed impregnable as ever. In twenty years the smooth shaft of granite had yielded to only three ascents. Despite our record of failures, I continued to hope for a brief window of calm weather. Just two successive good days would allow us to complete the fourth ascent.

Patagonia has a way of eating up time; as Christmas approached I became melancholy, knowing home was 11,000 kilometers away. I blotted our mission in the Paine Towers from my mind and immersed myself in memories of holidays past. The large gathering of families, the warm spirit and cheerful faces made my eyes damp. And the aromas! My nose twitched when I thought of the mince pies, mashed potatoes, gravy, turkey and stuffing. Bobby and I had one link with Christmas, a box of *Stove Top* stuffing mix. We prepared it over a small fire and ate in silence. I wondered if I were being selfish by not being home with my family. Would they think I cared for nothing but mountains anymore or would they understand? I vowed to be with them next year.

One week after Christmas we mustered up enough energy to plod back up to the split boulder at the glacier's edge to wait for a break in the weather. We excavated a hollow under the big rock with our ice hammers as the wind whipped gravel back and forth. Two walls of piled stones formed a ventilated partition between the ceiling and the floor. The wind, challenged by our tactics, forced the finer pieces of rock and sand into our shelter. Our faces had deep creases from the combination of anxiety, wind and sun. Bobby's hair stood out in every direction. Our clothing and hands were patched with tape. I tried to visualize our appearance in another week: two madmen sitting under a boulder playing with rocks while mumbling "tower big, wind strong, no food, tired, we leave".

I fell asleep dreaming of home and woke hearing nothing. The wind had stopped, four Andean condors circled above our camp. To me the birds were a symbol of hope but Bobby took them for the hungry vultures they were and tried to look inconspicuous. I reminded him that the birds only fed off dead creatures, as long as he appeared alive there was no reason to fret. We loaded our small rucksacks with a butane stove, two freeze dried dinners, instant tea, chocolate and a handful of dried fruit. In addition to the clothing we wore, we each carried a pile jacket and a couple of liters of water. From repeated failures we had learned that our bivouac tent, sleeping bags and several days of food were useless burdens. Only if we climbed quickly was there a slim chance of making it.

That evening we reached the ledge where one month before we had spent that harrowing night. It was perfectly calm. As the sun dipped toward Paine Grande in the west, the rich brown walls of the Fortress dropped into a deep shadow. We both felt happy for once and didn't care what the weather was about to do. "This is the last time I'm climbing up here", I said. Bobby huddled over the hissing stove, melting chunks of ice for dinner water.
"Yeah, I've had it too. The wind will probably start to blow any minute now and we'll be finished."

During the night the wind came up as we shivered and slept fitfully. The breeze was constant but did not intensify. Thin clouds crept toward us from the Patagonian Ice Cap as my mind reeled. The weather had conditioned us so well that, the instant we saw the tiniest cloud, we accepted defeat. "We're done for," I thought, but as it grew light my attitude changed; I hoped that the strong winds would hold off for another 24 hours. Silently, we ate breakfast and began climbing. Three pitches above the ledge Bobby said,"I don't like this weather. What do you think we should do?" Translated, that meant "Let's go down". My reply surprised him. "I'm not going down until the wind blows me off this mountain!"

The sun came out as I wedged fingers and toes into a thin crack, climbing to the high point of our second attempt in early December. I remembered leaving behind two small wired stoppers connected with twelve millimeter webbing for the rappel anchor. I recalled that the placements were very solid; they held my full 62 kilos as I descended. However, the two anchors were gone; there was only one explanation, the wind. It was sobering to think the wind could have enough force to rip those stoppers right out of the wall. I fixed my rope for Bobby to jumar and wriggled my cramped toes on the eight centimeter wide ledge. Across the col the curving granite blade of the South Tower dominated the panorama. In the distance I could see the black slate capping the Cuernos and puffy white clouds everywhere.

Four dark shapes soared through the portal formed by the two towers of rock. My eyes widened as the Andean condors glided to within five meters of the wall. The immature birds cocked their feathered heads back and forth, inspecting us curiously. Above me, Bobby had taken the lead and had become stymied by a short overhanging crack. As he didn't seem to be moving or showing much life at the time, the huge birds of prey became more interested as they rode the air currents to a point three meters from him. I was snapping pictures furiously while shouting encouragement to Bobby. "Wow, isn't this great? You've almost got it!" He grunted and wheezed, flapped his arms and legs and flopped on a sloping ledge. Bobby had finished his lead; the condors, seeing their potential prey was very much alive, soared away.

Our race against the fading light became frantic. We thought the climbing might ease off in one more rope length, but on a mountain of that size it was difficult to tell. Often what appeared to be a ledge was a sloping ramp, the gentler slopes turned out to be smooth and often holdless. We had climbed higher than on any previous attempt; the hope of success spurred me to move faster. For fifty meters I jammed hands and feet into a smooth crack on a vertical wall. The rope tightened; I yelled at Bobby to replace his belay anchors higher, so I could have enough rope to reach a ledge. For once I was not disappointed, I could stand comfortably on a good ledge. I anchored the rope and gave myself a little slack to move around freely.

The sun had gone down below the ice cap; night was upon us but we left our rucksacks, extra pitons and nuts on the ledge and began groping our way toward the summit in the dark. The moon glowed faintly through an overcast sky, barely illuminating boulders and ledges. The wind was blowing again; I suggested we huddle on the leeward side of a huge boulder to wait for dawn. There remained several steep pitches to the top that could not be climbed in the dark. My sweat soaked socks had robbed my feet of warmth, Bobby rubbed them back to life. In turn, I massaged his feet. Without any food or bivouac gear, this was our only means to prevent freezing.

At 5 am we traversed across ice slabs by chopping steps with our alpine hammers. Bobby led a mixed pitch of ice and rock that ended on a narrow ridge, where I grabbed the hardware from him and hurried toward the summit. The wind speed picked up; though I felt like rushing I kept a firm grip on the small rock knobs that supported my weight. My heart pounded with excitement as I found myself staring straight into the eyes of a fifteen centimeter high lead statue of the Madonna. The figurine had been stuffed into a crack on the summit almost twenty years before by an Italian expedition.

I stood up and screamed, "Off belay!" to Bobby below. The wind tugged at his anorak as he followed my moves to the top. Our eyes swept the horizon, identifying the mountains, lakes and glaciers. "There's Lago Dickson but where's Fitz Roy?" I shouted, above the deafening roar. Bobby forced a weak smile but his eyes revealed the extreme hardships of our six week effort to climb the Tower. His seamed face expressed one thought, "I want this ordeal to end!" Although the uncertain descent with its seventeen rappels still faced us, I knew we would survive. Right then I could not laugh or cry but sometime later, when we both were safe, I would indulge my emotions.

To the Italian figurine and the piton left by the British in 1963, we added an aluminum *Hexentric* with our names and the date scratched on it. A total of nine climbers had set foot on the summit in the years before. Although determination had played a major role in their success, and our victory, I was beginning to believe that luck also had a lot to do with it.

8

WILDNESS

Patagonia's wildness does not exist because of the inaccessibility of its spires; they can be reached along gentle trails. Nor because of the rarified air; the highest summit of the three groups in this book is a modest 3440 meters. It comes instead from the fearsom weather that, for weeks on end, can seal off the peaks with ice and raging winds. In his book, *Filming the Impossible,* Leo Dickinson described how the climate has kept people away. "The treacherous weather has guarded these mountains from attaining a degree of popularity enjoyed by the Himalaya and other equally remote ranges."

Although, along with the weather, the awesome walls have afforded a measure of protection against overuse, these faces are increasingly less of a deterrent, because of bolder and more skillful climbers and technical advancements in equipment. From 1959 to 1986, Cerro Torre was scaled 21 times. In just the 1987-88 season, it was climbed eight times by German, French, American, Austrian and Italian teams. Three of the expeditions included a woman, each of whom made the summit.

Photographs of the Fitz Roy and Paine mountains may attract mountaineers but the armor of terrible weather still remains the greatest obstacle and the mountains' most effective defensive weapon. Many climbers continue to choose sunnier climates, with a high ratio of climbing to stormbound days. Even so, interest in the area is growing.

Greater numbers of humans in mountain environments always have an effect, often deleterious The mountain's hard granitic rock can endure for millions of years but its pristine state will gradually erode as garbage at the base and ragged fixed ropes increase. Clearly, alpine-style climbing has less impact because small groups do not rely on a lot of rope and established camps. But a long lineup of parties, no matter how small, waiting to get on the routes, or multiple parties on the same route can have an identical result on the wilderness experience. Cerro Torre, Fitz Roy and the Towers of Paine might become backyard crags, festooned with climbing routes a few meters apart. Just as much as we need crags on which to practice, we need pristine mountains on which to exercise our alpine skills. Apart from the changes wreaked on the mountains, the civilized world threatens the surrounding environment.

The juggernaut of development continues to subdue the wilds of Patagonia. In Los Glaciares Park, a recently completed bridge over the Río Fitz Roy allows local ranchers easier access to their estancias and climbers and trekkers a safer trip into the mountains. In hopes of attracting people who might settle, the Argentine government also financed construction of a second hotel across the Río Fitz Roy from the existing hotel and a dozen resort dwellings. Patagonia is no longer a corner of the world where time stands still.

Wild places are necessary to maintain a quality life on this planet and only when they are gone, or altered, do people grieve their loss. George Simpson in **Attending Marvels** felt the need to preserve Patagonia fifty years ago. "It is good to think that there are some parts of the earth that may be destined never to be populous or civilized. A thoroughly subdued planet would be dull, and it would degenerate. I think mankind needs Patagonia as a permanent outpost, as a sort of museum specimen of the raw earth. I should like to transfer to such a place, a few at a time, those descendants of our pioneers who now complain if they have to leave concrete roads."

On my first expedition to Patagonia in 1981, my partner and I camped in the Río Ascencio Valley below the East Face of the Central Tower of Paine. The base camp had one fire ring, a broken pressure cooker pot and a small garbage pit with several tin cans scattered about. There were no other climbing expeditions in the entire valley. In 1990 I returned to the Paine group to attempt the Fortress and hiked through the same base camp.

I was unable to identify the exact spot we had erected our tent nine years before. Three makeshift log huts crowded the forest as did a dozen nylon tents. Expeditions from Germany, France and Spain were hard at work fixing rope on the Central Tower and Nido Negro de Condores. Members of one expedition were so intimidated by the weather, and so determined to go home victorious, that they borrowed additional fixed rope and anchored lines to within fifty meters of the summit of the Central Tower (1066 meters of rope in all). They cleaned most of the rope but left a heap of it lying on a ledge. After much route preparation, the leader finally admitted that a subsequent party would probably not be able to free the climb on sight either because the cracks would be filled with ice. Sport alpinism is here.

What I fear most for Patagonia's mountains is that the weather may no longer protect them. I have always felt that if people can't climb a route in good style and leave it unblemished for the next party, it is better not to climb it at all. After all, the most powerful image of a wild mountain is one that has never been scaled.

PLANNING AN EXPEDITION TO PATAGONIA

The short approaches and superb granite of Patagonia's mountains make the peaks very attractive to climbers. Although the weather is virtually unpredictable, porters are unnecessary and many fine routes can be accomplished in one to three days without a great deal of equipment. By sharing some of my experiences with mountain selection, permits, seasons, partners, language, travel, transportation, fuel, food and approaches; I hope to eliminate at least some of the problems facing a newcomer.

Mountain selection

The striking beauty of Cerro Torre, the massive walls of Fitz Roy or the elegant lines on the Towers of Paine are excellent choices for the climber interested in world class routes. These mountains are two or three day climbs, depending on the route. Numerous other peaks can be climbed in a single day, with possibly one bivouac. Aguja St. Exupéry, Aguja Rafaél (Innominata), Aguja Guillaumet, Aguja de la S, North Tower of Paine and the Cuernos del Paine fall into the latter category. Those interested in less technical scrambles can try Cerro Solo, Velluda, Cerro Eléctrico and Cerro Almirante Nieto. Climbers can reach most of the base camps in one day and high camp in one more day. Trails lead up the valleys to where the beech forests end and talus slopes or gentle glaciers complete the approach.

Route information is not readily available; in Appendix III, I have included three topos of the popular classic routes of the area. Some specific route information can be obtained from the *Alpine Journal,* the *American Alpine Journal, Climbing, Mountain* magazine and *Patagonia: Terra Magica Per Alpinisti e Viaggiatori (Magic Land for Climbers and Travelers)* by Gino Buscaini and Silvia Metzeltin. Appendix II provides basic historical ascent data and references for all reported routes.

Permission to climb

Obtaining permission to climb in Chilean or Argentine Patagonia is not difficult. Argentina presently collects a nominal fee, Chile charges nothing. For either country, write to the addresses below and tell them exactly where you plan to climb, your itinerary and how long you will spend in the country. Submit the names of the expedition members along with each one's address, age, occupation, marital status, passport number, nationality, club affiliation, climbing experience and doctor's certificate. For the Chilean authorities, a typed letter in Spanish is adequate; in 1990 they also required notarized photo copies of all passports. The Argentine Parks Department sends back an official form to fill out, it requires the same information.

Climbers have arrived in the Fitz Roy park without written permission, simply checked in with the Guardaparque (ranger) and done their climb. However, the governments of South American countries can be unpredictable. In 1972 the Argentine Parks Department insisted a British group obtain official permission before attempting a new route on Fitz Roy. The four climbers waited in dismay as nearly two weeks of perfect weather slipped by.

Current addresses for the two countries are:

> Servicio National,
> Parques National,
> Santa Fe 690,
> Buenos Aires, Argentina;
>
> El Director, Ministerio De Fronteral y Limites Del Estado,
> Santiago, Chile.

Season

The climbing season runs from October (mid spring) through late February (end of summer). October is colder with more snow on the glaciers and mountains. Temperatures increase as summer arrives, glaciers melt down to bare ice, making travel safer and easier. A pair of short mountaineering skis or snowshoes can be well worth taking along when planning an early expedition.

Heavy snowfall and lower temperatures can occur any time during the summer season; it's anyone's guess what controls the weather coming across the ice cap. Expect the unexpected and you won't be surprised. During the 1984-85 season, Bobby Knight and I anticipated only two to three days of climbing weather each month. Instead we were treated to sixteen straight days of clear and windless skies. Temperatures ranged from about -9° C at night to 21° C during the day.

Our choice of route on Fitz Roy (the North Pillar) turned out to be the only safe one, as the consecutive days of fine weather melted ice deep in cracks and behind blocks. House-sized chunks of granite went crashing down the other routes, making climbing very risky. All conditions should be anticipated on your chosen routes, from bare dry rock to snow, verglas or rime ice.

Partners

If, after arriving in the mountains and confronting the abominable weather, your chosen partner does not share your enthusiasm, you could be facing a solo climb or a wasted trip. It is far more important to go there with someone you get along with, rather than choosing team members according to their climbing ability. Triple digit climbers (5.10 ability and higher) may only function well on warm dry rock without a pack on. If you hose the rock with snow and ice and give them a 20 kilo pack, their performances can plummet drastically.

Small groups of two climbers are even more dependent on communication to deal with problems. When confined to a snow cave for even only two or three days, compatibility is a must.

Language

Before leaving home, I attempted to study Spanish, as there are very few English-speaking people in Patagonia. Voicing your needs to the Argentines or Chileans in their native language will reduce hassles and shorten the time required to reach the mountains.

A rudimentary way to communicate in Spanish is to make up your own small notebook of commonly used nouns, verbs and verb conjugations. In this way you can put together a sentence that will convey your message. Spend a little extra effort and look up the Spanish equivalents in a dictionary for your essential needs; special foods, stove fuel, horses, etc. If time permits, taking a Spanish course is highly recommended.

Travel tips

Check on the innoculations required and recommended for both countries, update your passport and apply for a visa well in advance of leaving. As of 1991, a visa was required for Argentina but not Chile. It is also an excellent idea to take along a photo copy of your passport, visa and list of valuables; in case the items are stolen or the parks or military officials decide to examine what you are bringing into their country.

Transportation

The most expensive item is generally air fare, which currently ranges from $1100 to $1650, depending on your city of origin. In Chile, flights are available from Santiago to Punta Arenas (included in total cost above) and from there a bus ($6.50 one way) heads north to Puerto Natales. From Puerto Natales during October and November, it is necessary to hire a taxi ($50 one way per person) or hitch a ride the ninety-odd kilometers to the mountains. In December tourist buses are running and cost less than half the fare of a taxi. In Puerto Natales there is a tour bus company next to Victoria Sur that runs trips to the Torres del Paine park ($7.50 one way).

In 1990 we also spent $70 apiece for a jeep ride and horses to transport our gear into the Río Ascencio Valley. In Argentina, flights connect the major cities Buenos Aires and Río Gallegos; then a bus ($11 one way) or a local flight with LADE Airlines ($14 one way) ends at Calafate. From Calafate, it is the same procedure as in Chile. Hire a taxi if you arrive early or take a bus later in the season. In 1988 it cost us about $12 apiece for horses to carry our gear to the Torre base camp.

Prices are variable in both countries because of the rapidly fluctuating economy. During 1981-82 prices were two and a half times higher in Chile than in the US, while in Argentina 1984-85, the costs ran about the same as in the US. In 1990 food and transportation within Chile was cheaper than in the US. If possible, try to contact someone who has just returned from Patagonia for information on current prices.

The pace of life is slower in Argentina and Chile. Merchants close shops at midday and generally function with less efficiency than Americans are accustomed to. Argentines, for example, deal with transportation problems in peculiar ways, as the American climber Jim Bridwell discovered in 1978. He was travelling in a bus that broke down many kilometers from help. The driver casually waited for another vehicle. When a second bus arrived, the drivers evacuated the women and children from the stricken vehicle and the working bus pushed the disabled one. Often reaching speeds of ninety kilometers an hour, the powerless bus drifted from one side of the road to the other, as its male occupants gripped the seats in terror.

Fuel

Obtaining fuel for cooking can be a challenge. In Chile we burned regular automobile gas in my heavy *Phoebus* stove while staying in caves, and for some base camp cooking. There is deadwood available in the forest for cook fires and it is acceptable to have fires, so long as people don't start chopping down green trees. Up on the mountain we used a *Husch* stove with propane-butane cartridges. One 200 ml cannister would produce five quarts of water from snow and ice.

In Argentina we again brought along the *Phoebus*. It happily burned automobile "super" but after a couple of weeks the *MSR Nine* fuel stove was not digesting "super" very well; halfway up Fitz Roy, the stove died. An abandoned *Husch* and borrowed cartridges from base camp did the job and joined me on Cerro Torre. Wrapping an aluminum windscreen around the *Husch* doubles its efficiency and if using a *Bluet*, it would be wise to make or obtain a copper tube double boiler that returns heat back down to the butane cannister. White gas is very difficult to find. However, in 1987 two American climbers did manage to locate white gas at a paint and marine supply shop at 877 Errazuriz in Punta Arenas.

In 1990 we obtained white gas at the Errazuriz address and in Ferrateria Aguila, a hardware store in the same town. Using the cone-shaped filters on the fuel intake tubes of *MSR GK's* and *Whisperlites* seemed to help. We also found 200mm and 750mm *Primus* butane cannisters available; those fit *Primus* and *Husch* stoves.

Food

Purchasing food is not a problem but two factors determine whether you should bring it all with you or buy it in Patagonia. If the exchange rate is not favorable and baggage allowances are high, bring your food with you; except for perishables such as cheese, salami and margarine. When the exchange rate is good and your baggage allowance is low, plan to buy everything in Punta Arenas or Río Gallegos.

In 1984 we brought along some freeze-dried food and purchased the remaining items from three supermarkets in Río Gallegos. There seemed to be a poor selection of good cookies or fig bars for munching and there wasn't any peanut butter. I enjoy buying a few basic ingredients, from which I can prepare many tasty entrées. With flour, baking powder and salt you can make tortillas, enchiladas, biscuits, cobbler and pizza; with yeast you can bake bread; and with sugar and eggs you can make pancakes, cookies and cake. Up in the mountains, the Prickly Heath berries were ripe and made a nice addition to many meals.

We bought a good supply of fresh potatoes, eggs and onions in Calafate and carried them the ten kilometers into the Fitz Roy base camp. It's hard to beat fried spuds and eggs for the first week or two; when guests stop by you can tantalize them with a real meal instead of something from an aluminum package. For Christmas, we baked several small canned hams peppered with cloves, over which we dribbled a sweet sauce spiced with *Old Smugglers* (Argentine whiskey). Boiled potatoes and sweetbread completed the meal.

Expenses for our 1990-91 expedition to Chile (per person)

Round trip air fare (Seattle to Punta Arenas via Miami and Santiago)	1640.00
Excess baggage	105.00
Transportation in Chile	160.00
Food for eight weeks	207.00
Fuel	18.00
Hotels and meals	350.00
Total	$2,480.00

Routes and approachs

Gravel roads lead to the edge of the mountains and allow easy access to hiking trails. The national parks of Chile and Argentina contain a network of trails that make travel easier. Fitz Roy and Cerro Torre occupy a small portion of the large Argentine national park called Los Glaciares. The Towers of Paine are included in the Chilean park known as Parque Nacional Torres del Paine. Most of the climbing, trekking and sightseeing takes place in these two parks.

My preference, when planning a climb, has been to pick routes that can be mostly free climbed and done quickly. Fixed rope is a nuisance and I take only 100 meters for the bergschrund at the mountain's base. Fixed ropes suffer from rockfall and wind abrasion and cannot always be trusted.

Choosing where to camp during stormy weather must be given serious thought. A snow cave puts you close to the mountain and ready for rapid action when the wind stops blowing. Cave life can be awfully lethargic and unless you move about, the idea of climbing anything after sitting, eating and sleeping for a week may be repugnant. At Col Superior on Fitz Roy, there is a deep snowbank for locating a cave. Small crags which rise above the col enable one to boulder fifty meters from the cave door. Shovelling snow and using a hand gripper also combat inactivity.

If the approach from the beech forest to the base of the route is not too bad, it is practical to camp in the forest and then dash up to the mountain when the barometer goes up and the clouds disappear. Down below you can hike, carry and chop wood, talk with other climbers and of course exercise your culinary skills. Both mind and body seem to remain healthier when not confined within the damp walls of a snow cave.

Final thoughts

Patagonia is not the place to go if reaching the summit is your most important goal. Failure can be very frustrating. Hike around the lakes, smell the flowers, go birdwatching, run up the hillsides, boulder, read those thick novels you brought along and enrich your experience by absorbing the surroundings. Should you succeed in reaching a summit or just get in some good climbing, your trip has an even greater potential for etching itself into your memory.

PEAKS AND ASCENTS, 1916-1991

This listing of first ascents and new routes completed in Patagonia extends from Mt San Valentín in the north to Monte Burney in the far south. As in the text and maps, peak names are those in common usage; English versions follow the Spanish names, where appropriate, to help the reader track down peak information in other sources. The route ascended by the climbing party and the date they reached the summit has been included wherever possible. Following the peak name and elevation are (in parentheses) the designation of the region and the name of the group to which the peak belongs. Only routes where one or more climbers reached the summit, and only those members of the expedition that made the top are listed.

This appendix would have been very difficult to compile without the extensive research accomplished by Gino Buscaini and Silvia Metzeltin, his wife. For their 1987 Patagonia book, they gleaned valuable first ascent information from Argentine climbing journals in Buenos Aires. Apart from the Buscainis' book *Patagonia: Terra Magica per Alpinisti e Viaggiatori. The Alpine Journal* and the *American Alpine Journal* provided additional and up to date route information.

Journal references are cited in the following form; volume or issue number, (year), page(s). References to the Buscainis' book are indicated by *PMLTM* followed by the page number(s). Other abbreviations used include:

AAJ:	*American Alpine Journal,*
	American Alpine Club, New York
AJ:	*Alpine Journal,* The Alpine Club, London
CL:	*Climbing Magazine,* Carbondale, CO
pc:	personal communication
N:	North
S:	South
W:	West
E:	East
FA:	First Ascent
NR:	New Route
m:	meters
NPI:	North Patagonian Ice Cap
SPI:	South Patagonian Ice Cap

Aguja Bifida - 2450m *(SPI, Cerro Torre, Cordón Adela)* P von Kanel, H P Trachsel, 1975; FA of lower (south) summit from col on Cerro Stanhardt, *AAJ 20 (1976) 504; PMLTM 228* H Bresba, P Luthi, 2 Mar 1989; NR via N face, *AAJ 32 (1990) 206*

Aguja Cuatro Dedos - 2245m *(SPI, Cerro Torre, Cordón Adela)* R Carrington, A Rouse, 24 Jan 1977; FA, *AAJ 21 (1978) 582; PMLTM 228*

Aguja de la S - 2350m *(SPI, Fitz Roy)* B Amy and three companions, Feb 1968; FA from E, *PMLTM 228* G C Grassi, R Pe, M Rossi, 30 Nov 1986; NR via W face H Barenthaler, E Lidl, Dec 1987; NR via E face, *AAJ 30 (1988) 175* M Sevilevski, V Trenev, 1989; NR via ESE face, *AAJ 32 (1990) 210*

Aguja de la Silla - 2978m *(SPI, Fitz Roy)* H Bresba, P Luthi, 21 Feb 1989; FA via E spur, *AAJ 32 (1990) 206*

Aguja Guillaumet - 2539m *(SPI, Fitz Roy)* C Comesaña, J L Fonrouge, 12 Jan 1965; FA via NW buttress, *PMLTM 221* J Coqueugniot, F Guillot, 26 Feb 1968; NR via E face center, *PMLTM 222* B Amy, P Vidailhet, 27 Feb 1968; NR via E face right, *PMLTM 222* R Beager, J Jennings, 10 Mar 1979; NR via SE face, *AAJ 22 (1980) 598-599; PMLTM 222* E Brenner, E Moschioni, 21 Jan 1981; NR via NE ridge, *PMLTM 223* G Buscaini, Silvia Metzeltin, 27 Dec 1981; NR via E face left side, *AAJ 25 (1983) 211; PMLTM 223* D Anker, T Wüschner, 8 Dec 1983; NR via E face extreme left side, *AAJ 26 (1984) 219; PMLTM 224* D Anker, M Piola, 12 Jan 1989; NR via SE face, *AAJ 32 (1990) 208*

Aguja Mermoz - 2754m *(SPI, Fitz Roy)* H Cuiñas, F Olaechea, G Vieiro, 10 Feb 1974; FA via NW face and N ridge, *PMLTM 221* J Jeglic, S Karo and F Knez, 9 Dec 1983; NR via E face left side, *AAJ 26 (1984) 219* A Columbo, G Confalonieri, D Corbetta, D Galbiati, G Maggioni, V Spinnelli, E Tanzi, 31 Oct 1989; NR via E buttress, *AAJ 32 (1990) 208-209*

Aguja Poincenot - 3036m *(SPI, Fitz Roy)* F Cochrane, D Whillans, 3 Feb 1962; FA via E face and upper SE ridge, *AJ 67 (1962) 236-242; PMLTM 224* J L Fonrouge, A Rosasco, 21 Dec 1968; NR via SW face, *PMLTM 224* J L Fonrouge, A Rosasco, 17-21 Dec 1970; NR via NW face; *AAJ 18 (1973) 477* R Carrington, A Rouse, 22 Feb 1977; NR via W face; *AAJ 21 (1978) 583; PMLTM 225* D Bosisio, M Panzeri, M D Santa, P Vitali, 7 Dec 1986; NR via WNW face, *PMLTM 226* D Anker, M Piola, 9 Jan 1989; NR on upper E face, *AAJ 32 (1990) 208*

Aguja Pollone - 2260m *(SPI, Fitz Roy)* R Smithers, C Ward, 23 Feb 1976; FA via S face, *AAJ 21 (1977) 231; PMLTM 213*

Aguja Rafaél (Torre Innominata) - 2501m *(SPI, Fitz Roy)* M Boysen, P Braithwaite, L Dickinson, D Reid, R Sylvester, Feb 1974; FA via W face and SW ridge, *AAJ 20 (1975) 184-188; PMLTM 226* D Anker, M Piola, 6 Jan 1989; NR via N spur, *AAJ 32 (1990) 208*

Aguja Saint Exupéry - 2680m *(SPI, Fitz Roy)* G Buscaini, L Candot, Silvia Metzeltin, W Romano, S Sinigoi, 23 Feb 1968; FA via E buttress, *AAJ 16 (1969) 448; PMLTM 226* M Giordani, Rosanna Manfrini, S Valentini, 5 Nov 1988; NR via W face, *AAJ 31 (1989) 176* H Barenthaler, E Lidl, Dec 1987; NR via S pillar, *AAJ 29 (1987) 175* Sue Harrington, A Kearney, 10 Feb 1988; NR via N face and upper E ridge, *AAJ 31 (1989) 176-178*

Aguja Volonqui - 2100m *(SPI, Cordón Marconi)* R Carrington, A Rouse, 17 Dec 1976, FA via NE buttress *AAJ 21 (1977) 581-583; AJ 83 (1978) 582; PMLTM 210*

Aleta del Tiburón (Shark's Fin) - 1850m *(SPI, Paine)* G Casassa, C Cognian, J Pardo, G Salamanca, Jan 1978; FA via W face, *PMLTM 252* G Bonneville, M Ignat, Denise Ravaine, 2 Jan 1982; NR via S ridge *AAJ 25 (1983) 212-213; PMLTM 252* J Bald, P Simmons, Jan 1982; NR via E face *PMLTM 252*

Cabeza del Indio (Indian's Head) - 2230m *(SPI, Paine)* Y Astier, J M Boucansoud, J J Jaouen, J F Lemoine, Nov 1981; FA from S, *PMLTM 252*

Cachu - 2600m *(NPI, San Valentin, Arenales)* H Hess, W Schmitt, 16 Jan 1940; FA, *PMLTM 186*

Cerro Adela Central - 2960m *(SPI, Cerro Torre, Cordón Adela)* W Bonatti, C Mauri, 7 Feb 1958; FA via gully on WSW side, *PMLTM 233*

Cerro Adela Sur - 2860m *(SPI, Cerro Torre, Cordón Adela)* W Bonatti, C Mauri, 7 Feb 1958; FA via traverse from NW to S, *PMLTM 233* L Eccher, C Maestri, 1958; NR via S ridge. *PMLTM 233* J Aikes, N Monaco, O Pellegrini, 2 Mar 1967; NR via NE ridge, *PMLTM 233* G C Grassi, M Rossi, 10 Dec 1986; NR via NE face, *PMLTM 233*

Cerro Agassiz - 2940m *(SPI, Murallón, Roma)* G Mengelle, P Skvarca, Jan 1966; FA, *PMLTM 242*

Cerro Agudo - 2600m *(NPI, San Valentin, Arenales)* P Gresham, G Vickers, R Vickers, 8 Jan 1970; FA via S ridge, *AAJ 17 (1971) 429-430; PMLTM 186*

Cerro Anders *(SPI, Cerro Campana, Cerro Norte)* R Czerniawski, P Skvarca, 4 Feb 1971; FA, *PMLTM 236*

Cerro Arco - 3012m *(NPI, San Valentin, Arenales)* E Garcia, M Gomez, C Marangunic, E Shipton, 25 Dec 1963; *AJ 69 (1964) 183-190; PMLTM 186*

Cerro Arenales - 3437m *(NPI, San Valentin, Arenales)* Clausen, Emmanji, Taga-ki, 6 Mar 1958; AJ 63 (1958) 259; *PMLTM 186*

Cerro Arido - 2250m *(E of NPI, San Lorenzo)* L Herold, E Parusel, 6 Feb 1955; FA from NW, *PMLTM 194*

Cerro Aspero - 2075m *(E of NPI, San Lorenzo)* E Parusel, 13 Feb 1955; FA from SE, *PMLTM 194*

Cerro Astillado - 1746m *(SPI, San Martin, O'Higgins)* A Aste, F Defrancesco, M Mànica, M Marisa, 22 Jan 1985; FA via SW face, *AJ 91 (1986) 206; PMLTM 204*

Cerro Balmaceda - 2035m *(SPI, Mano del Diablo, Balmaceda)* I Arnsek, C Bo-tazzi, O Meiling, M Saavedra, 8 Nov 1957; FA, *AAJ 11 (1958) 103; PMLTM 261*

Cerro Bertrand - 3170m *(SPI, Murallón, Roma)* J & P Skvarca, Jan 1966; FA from E, *PMLTM 242*

Cerro Blanco - 2600m *(SPI, Mano del Diablo, Balmaceda)* G MacSweeney, 26 Feb 1976; FA, *AJ 74 (1969) 276; PMLTM 260*

Cerro Boj - 2700m *(SPI, Cerro Campana, Cerro Norte)* M Serrano, J Skvarca, 9 Jan 1969; FA, *PMLTM 237*

Cerro Cagliero - 2570m *(SPI, Piramide, Gorra Blanca)* A Mengelle, P Skvarca, 12 Jan 1964; FA from SW, *PMLTM 208*

Cerro Campana - 2750m *(SPI, Cerro Campana, Cerro Norte)* M Serrano, J Skvarca, 18 Feb 1968; FA from W, *PMLTM 236*

Cerro Castillo - 2675m *(E of NPI, Cerro Castillo)* R Aguilera, O Latorre, A Marcel, G Oyarzún, 10 Feb 1966; FA via W face, *AAJ 15 (1967) 399; PMLTM 188* T Golnar, L Hansel, C Kyan-Son, D Waugh, 5 Dec 1982; NR via SE face, *AAJ 26 (1984) 220; PMLTM 188*

Cerro Castillo - 2100m *(SPI, Paine)* F Arias, J Rivera, Feb 1980; FA via S face, *AJ 86 (1981) 234; PMLTM 251*

Cerro Cono - 2500m *(SPI, Murallón, Roma)* L Pera, J Skvarca, 20 Jan 1967; FA, *PMLTM 241*

Cerro Cota - 2000m *(SPI, Paine)* G Oyarzún, B Paul, J Quinteros, J Troncoso, Jan 1971; FA, *AAJ 17 (1971) 431-432; AJ 76 (1971) 248; PMLTM 251*

Cerro Cristál - 2200m *(SPI, Cerro Campana, Cerro Norte)* M Serrano, J Skvarca, 17 Feb 1968; FA, *PMLTM 236*

Cerro Cristal - 2600m *(NPI, San Valentin, Arenales)* A Bibby, B Gunn, D Launder, J Nankervis, 2 Jan 1970; FA via W ridge, *AJ 75 (1970) 224-230; PMLTM 183*

Cerro Cubo - 2920m *(SPI, Mayo, Cervantes, Cubo)* T Kadota, Y Onishi, K Terazawa, 1969; FA from N, *AAJ 27 (1985) 242; PMLTM 245*

Cerro Doblado - 2675m *(SPI, Cerro Torre, Cordón Adela)* C Detassis, C Maestri, M Stenico, 5 Feb 1958; FA from S, *PMLTM 233*

Cerro Don Bosco - 2515m *(SPI, Murallón, Roma)* E Klenk, A Pastewski, J Peterek, 3 Feb 1957; FA via E ridge, *AAJ 10 (1957) 101; PMLTM 241* G Alippi, B Balatti L Spadaccini, 8 Jan 1990: NR via S face, *AAJ 33 (1991) 191*

Cerro Dos Picos - 2275m *(E of NPI, San Lorenzo)* R Hoare, G Mosley, 1977; FA of E summit, *PMLTM 195* P Fatti, J Moss, G Pallister, R Smithers, 1980; FA of W summit, *PMLTM 195*

Cerro Eléctrico - 2182m *(SPI, Fitz Roy)* A De Agostini, M Derriard, Feb 1932; FA from the NE, *PMLTM 224* G Buscaini, Silvia Metzeltin, 8 Jan 1982; NR via W ridge, *PMLTM 224*

Cerro Feo - 2300m *(E of NPI, Cerro Castillo)* L Duff, N Groves, 9 Feb 1976; *AAJ 21 (1977) 235; PMLTM 188*

Cerro Ferrier - 1590m *(SPI, Mano del Diablo, Balmaceda)* P Alarcon, Esther Fuchs, 1985; *PMLTM 260*

Cerro Fiero - 3300m *(NPI, San Valentín, Arenales)* B Gunn, J Nankervis, 20 Dec 1969; FA via N ridge, *AJ 75 (1970) 224-230; PMLTM 183*

Cerro Grande - 2804m *(SPI, Cerro Torre, Cordón Adela)* C Detassis, C Maestri, M Stenico, 5 Feb 1958; FA from N, *PMLTM 233* W Bonatti, C Mauri, 7 Feb 1958; FA of W summit, *PMLTM 233*

Cerro Hermosa - 2500m *(E of NPI, San Lorenzo)* H Cuiñas, J Jason, G Vieiro, 1976; FA of main summit, *PMLTM 194*

Cerro Huemúl - 2750m *(SPI, Cerro Torre, Cordón Adela)* A Kölliker, F Kühn, L Witte, 23 Feb 1916; FA, *PMLTM 234*

Cerro Hyades - 3078m *(NPI, San Valentín, Arenales)* A Bibby, B Gunn, D Launder, J Nankervis, 7 Jan 1970; FA via N face, *AAJ 17 (1971) 429-430; PMLTM 186* T Clarkston, J Spearpoint, 15 Jan 1973; NR via SW ridge, *AAJ 19 (1974) 197; PMLTM 186*

Cerro Indeterminado *(SPI, San Martin-O'Higgins)* E Gebauerl, J Gertis, J Hardt, D Hirsch, 1962; FA, *PMLTM 204*

Cerro La Torre - 2900m *(NPI, San Valentín, Arenales)* A Bibby, B Gunn, D Launder, J Nankervis, 23 Dec 1969; FA via E ridge, *AJ 75 (1970) 224-230; PMLTM 183*

Cerro MacAndrews - 2800m *(SPI, Murallón, Roma)* J Salz, 1973; FA via NE ridge, *PMLTM 242*

Cerro Mano del Diablo *(SPI, Mano del Diablo, Balmaceda)* B Doligez, J L Hourcadette, 18 Jan 1987; FA, *AAJ 31 (1989) 179; PMLTM 260*

Cerro Marconi Central - 2257m *(SPI, Cordón Marconi)* E Köpcke, A Nacachian, E Triep, 14 Jan 1966; FA via W face, *PMLTM 210*

Cerro Marconi Norte - 1978m *(SPI, Cordón Marconi)* A Cazaux, J Guthmann, J Pillet, C Stegmann, G Watzl, 13 Feb 1952; FA, *PMLTM 210*

Cerro Mayo - 2450m *(SPI, Mayo, Cervantes, Cubo)* A De Agostini, L Bron, E Croux, E Feruglio, 5 Jan 1931; FA from N and via NNW ridge, *PMLTM 244* M Curnis, C Ferrari, S Dalla Longa, A Manganoni, 15 Dec 1984; NR via W ridge, *AAJ 27 (1985) 242; PMLTM 244-245*

Cerro Milanesio - 2010m *(SPI, Piramide, Gorra Blanca)* A De Agostini, C Cassera, A Zampieri, 1937; FA from N, *PMLTM 208*

Cerro Mimosa *(SPI, Cordón Lautaro)* M Coffey, L Dickinson, E Jones, 4 Mar 1973; FA via S ridge, *AAJ 19 (1974) 200*

Cerro Mocho - 2600m *(NPI, San Valentín, Arenales)* A Bibby, D Launder, J Nankervis, 2 Jan 1970; FA via SW ridge, *AAJ 17 (1971) 429-430; PMLTM 183*

Cerro Moreno - 3554m *(SPI, Cordón Mariano Moreno)* F Doro Altan, W Bonatti, R Eggmann, C Mauri, 4 Feb 1958; FA via E buttress, *PMLTM 209*

Cerro Moyano - 2720m *(SPI, Cerro Campana, Cerro Norte)* H Cuiñas, J Skvarca, G Vieiro, 2 Feb 1976; FA via N face and ridge, *PMLTM 237*

Cerro Ñato - 2808m *(SPI, Cerro Torre, Cordón Adela)* E Castiglioni, L Dubosc, T Gilberti, 8 Feb 1937; FA via SW ridge, *PMLTM 233* D Brighenti, A Rampini, 3-4 Nov 1987; NR via SSE spur, *AAJ 31 (1989) 176*

Appendix II

Cerro Norte - 2950m *(SPI, Cerro Campana, Cerro Norte)* J & P Skvarca, 5 Feb 1970; FA via W face, *PMLTM 237* C Ferrari, G Maresi, 1 Jan 1986; FA via E face, *AAJ 29 (1987) 212; PMLTM 237*

Cerro O'Higgins - 2910m *(SPI, San Martin, O'Higgins)* W Espinoza, E Garcia, C Marangunic, F Vivanco, 16 Jan 1960; FA via SW face, *AJ 65 (1960) 241-242; PMLTM 204*

Cerro Olguin - 2300m *(SPI, Paine)* T Matsuzawa, A Miyashita, K Shirokura, 19 Jan 1969; FA, *AJ 75 (1970) 236-236; PMLTM 248*

Cerro Ostrava - 2250m *(SPI, Paine)* V Sagan, J Tomcala, J Volny, 13 Feb 1969; FA, *AJ 75 (1970) 236; PMLTM 248*

Cerro Palo - 2320m *(E of NPI, Cerro Castillo)* L Duff, N Groves, 5 Feb 1976; *AAJ 21 (1977) 235; PMLTM 188*

Cerro Patrullera Villarica - 2133m *(SPI Mano del Diablo Balmaceda)* B Doligez, J L Hourcadette, R Hémon, M Roquefre, 16 Nov 1982; FA, *PMLTM 260*

Cerro Penitentes - 2943m *(E of NPI, San Lorenzo)* P Fatti, J Moss, G Pallister, R Smithers, 1980; FA from north, *PMLTM 193*

Cerro Peñon - 2035m *(E of NPI, Cerro Castillo)* D Waugh, 1982; *AAJ 26 (1984) 220; PMLTM 188*

Cerro Pier Giorgio - 2565m *(SPI, Fitz Roy)* J & P Skvarca, 17 Jan 1963; FA via SE face, *PMLTM 210* M Mànica, R Vettori, 22 Nov 1985; NR via NW pillar, *PMLTM 210-213*

Cerro Pintado - 2547m *(SPI, Cerro Campana, Cerro Norte)* H Barria, P Skvarca, 11 Feb 1968; FA, *PMLTM 237*

Cerro Piramide - 2700m *(E of NPI, San Lorenzo)* M Lynch, J Sorondo, 21 Feb 1972; FA from SE and via E ridge, *PMLTM 208* Cristina Agued, G Buscaini, Silvia Metzeltin, E Tarditti, 7 Jan 1987; FA from S, *PMLTM 193*

Cerro Planchón - 2450m *(SPI, Paine)* K Suzuki, T Takahashi, 1969; FA, *AJ 75 (1970) 236; PMLTM 247*

Cerro Pollone - 2396m *(SPI, Fitz Roy)* R Dangl, G Lantschner, R Matzi, H Zechner, 11 Feb 1949; FA from E side, *PMLTM 213*

Cerro Puntudo - 2061m *(E of NPI, Cerro Castillo)* R Aguilera, O Latorre, A Marcel, G Oyarzún, 1966; *AAJ 15 (1967) 399; PMLTM 188*

Cerro Q - 1980m *(E of NPI, San Lorenzo)* G Maioli, A Pietrelli, 6 Feb 1983; FA, *PMLTM 194*

Cerro Rincón - 2234m *(SPI, Cordón Marconi)* F Bosch, C Comesaña, A Fragueiro, I Palma, 23 Feb 1971; FA from NE, *PMLTM 210*

Cerro Riso Patrón - 3000m *(SPI, Riso Patrón)* C Ferrari, B Lombardi, E Spreafico, 15 Aug 1988; FA vla ESE face, *AAJ 31 (1989) 178*

Cerro Roma - 3270m *(SPI, Murallón, Roma)* M Serrano, J Skvarca, 3 Feb 1969; FA from NE, *PMLTM 242*

Cerro Siniolchu - 2400-2599m *(NPI, San Valentin, Arenales)* A Bibby, B Gunn, 8 Jan 1970; FA via N face and W ridge, *AJ 75 (1970) 224-230; PMLTM 183*

Cerro Solo - 2248m *(SPI, Cerro Torre, Cordón Adela)* R Matzi, E Sabatté, 13 Feb 1949; FA from the N, *PMLTM 234*

Cerro Stanhardt - 2800m *(SPI, Cerro Torre, Cordón Adela)* J Bridwell, G Smith, J Smith, Jan 1988; FA via E face and N ridge, pc, *AAJ 31 (1989) 57-65* M Giarolli, E Orlandi, E Salvaterra, 22 Sep 1989; NR via W face, *AAJ 32 (1990) 210*

Cerro Steffen - 3050m *(SPI, San Martin, O'Higgins)* J & P Skvarca, 28 Jan 1965; FA via E face to saddle between Cerro Steffen and Cerro Kruger, *PMLTM 203*

Cerro Stokes - 2140m *(SPI, Paine)* A Brooks, P Chapman, B Farmer, R McLeod, J Murrell, 7 Nov 1976; FA via S face, *AAJ 21 (1977) 233; PMLTM 247*

Cerro Torre - 3128m *(SPI, Cerro Torre, Cordón Adela)* T Egger, C Maestri, 31 Jan 1959; FA (?) via lower E face and upper N face, *AAJ 11 (1959) 317; PMLTM 230* D Chiappa, M Conti, C Ferrari, P Negri, 13 Jan 1974; NR via W face, *AAJ 19 (1974) 201; PMLTM 232* S Brewer, J Bridwell, 4 Jan 1979; first completion of SE ridge to the summit, *AAJ 22 (1980) 375-382; PMLTM 231* M Fistravec, J Jeglic, S Karo, F Knez, P Kozjek, P Podgornik, 16 Jan 1986; NR via E face, *AAJ 29 (1987) 114-122; PMLTM 233*

Cerro Tronco - 2500m *(NPI, San Valentín, Arenales)* H Hess, H Schmoll, 25 Dec 1945; FA from Cristal Pass, *PMLTM 183*

Cerro Turret - 2000m *(NPI, San Valentín, Arenales)* D Launder, J Nankervis, 8 Jan 1970; FA via E face, *AJ 75 (1970) 224-230; PMLTM 186*

Cerro Vespignani - 2200m *(SPI, Piramide, Gorra Blanca)* C Fava, B Kambic, 20 Jan 1968; FA, *PMLTM 208*

Cerro W - 2205m *(E of NPI, San Lorenzo)* G Maioli, A Pietrelli, 7 Feb 1983; FA, *PMLTM 194*

Cima Oggioni - 2200m *(SPI, Paine)* A Aste, I Saenz, 24 Jan 1966; FA, *PMLTM 258*

Cono Helado - 2400m *(NPI, San Valentín, Arenales)* A Bibby, B Gunn, D Launder, J Nankervis, 6 Jan 1970; FA via W ridge, *AJ 75 (1970) 224-230; PMLTM 183*

Cordón Riso Patrón, - 2950m *(SPI, Riso Patrón)* H Maekawa, M Matsunaga, 16 Feb 1969; FA (north summit), *AJ 75 (1970) 230-234; PMLTM 238*

Cuerno de Plata - 3850m *(NPI, San Valentín, Arenales)* P Gresham, D Launder, 20 Dec 1969; FA via S ridge, *AJ 75 (1970) 224-230; PMLTM 183*

Cuerno Central (Cuerno Principal) - 2100m *(SPI, Paine)* R Aguilera, E García, O Latorre, G Oyarzún, 31 Jan 1968; FA from N, *AJ 73 (1968) 157; PMLTM 254* D Asay, J Miller, R Smithers, Feb 1976; NR via S face, *AAJ 21 (1977) 68-72; PMLTM 254*

Cuerno Norte - 2000m *(SPI, Paine)* P Anderson, T Dick, P Fatti, R Fuggle, R Hoare, M Scott, 30 Dec 1971; FA, *AAJ 18 (1973) 330; PMLTM 254*

Dedo del César - 1900m *(SPI, Mayo, Cervantes, Cubo)* M Gonzalez, G Iglesias, J Pablo, 18 Feb 1978; FA, *PMLTM 245*

Desmochada *(SPI, Fitz Roy)* J Bridwell, G Dunmire, J Smith, 13 Feb 1988; FA via W face, *AAJ 31 (1989) 57-65*

Domo Blanco - 2315m *(SPI, Fitz Roy)* A Cazaux, J Guthmann, J Pillet, C Stegmann, G Watzl, 31 Jan 1952; FA via NW face, *PMLTM 210*

El Mocho - 1980m *(SPI, Cerro Torre, Cordón Adela)* J Bridwell, R Staszewski, 28 Feb 1978; FA via SE buttress, *AAJ 21 (1978) 583; PMLTM 233* G C Grassi, R Pe, M Rossi, 18 Nov 1986; NR via couloir on E side, *PMLTM 233* G C Grassi, R Pe, M Rossi, 7 Dec 1986; NR via E buttress, *PMLTM 233* J Jeglic, S Karo, F Knez, R Pe, 11 Dec 1986; NR via N face, *PMLTM 233* M Malgarotto, A Rampini, M Venzo, 28 Oct 1987; NR via E buttress left side, *AAJ 31 (1989) 176*

Escudo (Shield) - 2450m *(SPI, Paine)* M Curnis, M Dotti, 31 Jan 1968; FA via SW face, *PMLTM 253*

Espada (Sword) - 2050m *(SPI, Paine)* T Dick, P Fatti, R Fuggle, R Hoare, M Scott, 19-21 Dec 1971; FA via SW side, *AAJ 18 (1973) 330-332; PMLTM 253-254*

Fitz Roy - 3441m *(SPI, Fitz Roy)* G Magnone, L Terray, 2 Feb 1952; FA via lower E face and right side S buttress, *PMLTM 214* C Comesaña, J L Fonrouge, 16 Jan 1965; NR via the Supercouloir on WNW side, *AAJ 15 (1966) 75-80; PMLTM 214* Y Chouinard, D Dorworth, C Jones, L Tejada-Flores, D Tompkins, 20 Dec 1968; NR via SW ridge, *AAJ 16 (1969) 263-269; AJ 74*

(1969) 130-132; PMLTM 216 J M Anthoine, E Birch, G Lee, D Nicol, I Wade, 11 Dec 1972; NR via S buttress, *AAJ 18 (1973) 477; PMLTM 218* C Ferrari, V Meles, 23 Feb 1976; NR via E pillar *AAJ 21 (1977) 230-231; PMLTM 218* R Casarotto, 19 Jan 1979; NR via N pillar, *AAJ 22 (1980) 383-386; PMLTM 218* G Abert, J & M Afanassief, J Fabre, 27 Dec 1979; NR via NNW face, *AAJ 23 (1981) 238; PMLTM 218* R Gálfy, M Orolin, V Petrik, 15 Jan 1983; NR via W face, *AAJ 25 (1983) 209; AAJ 26 (1984) 69-74; PMLTM 218* A Bendinger, E Brenner, M Coach, P Friedrich, 10 Mar 1984; NR via direct S buttress, *AAJ 27 (1985) 36-40; PMLTM 220 W Burzynski, M Falco-Sasal, P Lutynski, M Kochanczak, J Kozaczkiewicz, 24 Dec 1984; NR via N face, AAJ 27 (1985) 240; PMLTM 220* B Biscak, R Fabjan, M Lenarcic, 22 Dec 1985; NR via S face, *AAJ 29 (1987) 109-113; PMLTM 220*

Fortaleza (Fortress) - 2700m *(SPI, Paine)* J Gregory, G Hibberd, D Nicol, 5 Jan 1968; FA of SW side and upper W ridge, *AJ 73 (1968) 143-157; PMLTM 253* F Bristot, R Cazan, B De Dona, 26 Nov 1989: NR via NE Spur, *AAJ 33 (1991) 201* M Lukic, M Praprotnik, 28 Dec 1990; NR via E face, pc

Gorra Blanca - 2920m *(SPI, Piramide, Gorra Blanca)* A Mengelle, P Skvarca, 12 Jan 1964; FA from Gorra Blanca Sur, then via SE face, *PMLTM 208* G Buscaini, Silvia Metzeltin, 18 Jan 1984; NR via NW ridge, *PMLTM 208*

Gran Gendarme del Pollone - 2200m *(SPI, Fitz Roy)* R Carrington, A Rouse, 15 Dec 1976; FA via SE corner, *AAJ 21 (1978) 581-583; PMLTM 213*

Hoja (Blade), - 1950m *(SPI, Paine)* Y Astier, J M Boucansaud, J J Jaouen, J F Lemoine, Dec 1981; FA via N Ridge, *PMLTM 254* D Boyrie, D Charron, J Comparat, J Pilon, A Rebreyrend, 5 Jan 1982; NR via W face, *AAJ 25 (1983) 212; PMLTM 254*

La Catedrál (Cathedral) - 2200m *(SPI, Paine)* C Jackson, G Lee, D Nicol, B Shaw, B Smith, R Whewell, 9 Jan 1971; FA via W ridge, *AJ 75 (1970) 234-235; PMLTM 251*

La Chimenea - 2085m *(E of NPI, San Lorenzo)* G Buscaini, Silvia Metzeltin, 20 Dec 1986; FA via E face, *PMLTM 195*

Loma Blanca - 2150m *(SPI, Fitz Roy)* A De Agostini, L Carrel, C Cassera, G Pellissier, Feb 1936; FA from NW side, *PMLTM 213*

Máscara (Mummer) - 1850m *(SPI, Paine)* D Cheesemond, P Dawson, 7 Dec 1976; FA via SW face, *AAJ 21 (1977) 234; PMLTM 254* D Boyrie, D Charron, J Comparat, J Pilon, A Rebreyrend, 10 Jan 1982; NR via S face, *AAJ 25 (1983) 212; PMLTM 254*

Mellizo Oeste (West Twin) - 2450m *(SPI, Paine)* J Bald, P Simmons, 26 Dec 1981; FA, *PMLTM 251*

Mojon Rojo - 2224m *(SPI, Fitz Roy)* S Bossini, C Fava, A Vincitorio, 4 Mar 1961; FA from E, *AAJ 12 (1961) 263; PMLTM 228* J Bridwell, R Staszewski, Mar 1977; NR via W face, *AAJ 21 (1978) 584; PMLTM 228*

Monte Burney - 1768m *(S of SPI, Sarmiento, Burney)* R Perry, P Radcliffe, E Shipton, 10 Mar 1973; FA, *AAJ 19 (1974) 129-130; PMLTM 261-262*

Monte Torino - 2252m *(SPI, Murallón, Roma)* A De Agostini, L Bron, E Croux, E Feruglio, 5 Feb 1931; FA, *PMLTM 242*

Murallón - 2831m *(SPI, Murallón, Roma)* C Aldè, C Ferrari, P Vitali, 14 Feb 1984; FA via NE buttress, *AJ 91 (1986) 220; PMLTM 241*

Nido Negro De Condores - 2100m *(SPI, Paine)* Y Boullen, P Faivre, L Pernollet, D Ravanel, J Ruby, 17 Dec 1990: FA via E face left side, *pc; AAJ 33 (1991) 201*

Paine Chico, Cima Este (Almirante Nieto) - 2670m *(SPI, Paine)* H Teufel, S Zuck, 7 Jan 1937; FA (east summit) via NNE ridge, *AAJ 3 (1938) 227; PMLTM 254* H Kaltschmidt, O Meiling, 15 Jan 1954; NR via E ridge, *PMLTM 254*

Paine Chico, Cima Oeste - 2530m *(SPI, Paine)* P Baudis, P Klimza, L Zahoransky, 13 Feb 1969; FA (west summit), *AJ 75 (1970) 236; PMLTM 254*

Paine Grande, Cima Central - 2730m *(SPI, Paine)* L Krahl, S Kunstmann, E Payá, R Vivanco, 11 Feb 1955; FA of central summit from W, *AJ 61 (1956-57) 398; PMLTM 249*

Paine Grande, Cima Norte - 2760m *(SPI, Paine)* Y Takeuchi, 30 Jan 1969; FA of north summit, *AJ 75 (1970) 235-236; PMLTM 249*

Paine Grande, Cima Principal - 3050m *(SPI, Paine)* J Bich, L Carrel, T Gobi, C Pelissier, P Pession, 27 Dec 1957; FA of main summit from S then upper E face to NE ridge, *AJ 63 (1958) - 259; PMLTM 249* J & H Davies, C Lomax, 9 Dec 1984; NR via E face, *PMLTM 249*

Paine Grande, Cima Sud (Punta Bariloche) - 2660m *(SPI, Paine)* T Pangerc, H Schmoll, Dec 1953; FA of south summit, *PMLTM 249*

Pico Sur - 3300m *(NPI, San Valentin, Arenales)* C Lucero, R Vickers, 24 Dec 1969; FA via E ridge, *AJ 75 (1970) 224-230; PMLTM 183*

Piramide Bella Vista - 2130m *(E of NPI, San Lorenzo)* G Buscaini, Silvia Metzeltin, 23 Jan 1985; FA, *PMLTM 194*

Punta Anna - 2050m *(SPI, Fitz Roy)* C Maestri, 2 Feb 1958; FA from Torre Glacier, *PMLTM 213*

Punta Casari - 2000m *(SPI, Monti del Fiordo Bernardo)* W Bonatti, M Foresti, E Sangiovanni, 27 Nov 1985; FA from SW and via SE side, *PMLTM 204*

Punta Catalina - 2100m *(SPI, Paine)* I Ibaceta, P Keller, G Oyarzún, 2 Jan 1982; FA via W ridge(?)

Punta Eboulis - 1750m *(SPI, Paine)* J & Jeannine Comparat, 10 Jan 1982; FA via N face, *AAJ 25 (1983) 212-213; PMLTM 253*

Punta Herron - 2780m *(SPI, Cerro Torre, Cordón Adela)* B De Donà, G Giongo, 15 Mar 1980; FA from S on descent from Torre Egger's summit, *PMLTM 229*

Punta Mujer - 2150m *(SPI, Fitz Roy)* C Maestri, 2 Feb 1958; FA from Torre Glacier, *PMLTM 213* Cristina Agued, Maria Ines Bustos, 20 Jan 1984; NR from N side, *PMLTM 213*

Punta Negra - 2100m *(SPI, Paine)* I Burgess, S Hillen, D Lister, D Tyson, 19 Oct 1989; FA via NW face and N ridge, *AAJ 32 (1990) 210*

Punta Quirquinchos - 2000m *(SPI, Paine)* G Bonneville, M Ignat, D Ravaine, 5 Jan 1982; FA via E couloir around to W face and via N ridge, *PMLTM 251*

Punta Val Biois *(SPI, Fitz Roy)* B De Donà, G Pagani, 8 Jan 1978; FA from chockstone on N Pillar of Fitz Roy, *PMLTM 221*

San Lorenzo, Cumbre Principal - 3706m *(E of NPI, San Lorenzo)* A De Agostini, A Hemmi, H Schmoll, 17 Dec 1943; FA of main summit via W side of N ridge, *PMLTM 192* H P Bokker, R Dodding, P Fatti, E Muller, 15 Jan 1986; NR via E ridge, *AAJ 29 (1987) 208-209; PMLTM 192*

San Lorenzo, Cumbre Sur - 3300m *(E of NPI, San Lorenzo)* G Buscaini, Silvia Metzeltin, 15 Jan 1986; FA of south summit via S face and W ridge, *AAJ 29 (1987) 207-208; PMLTM 192-193*

San Lorenzo, Hombro Norte - 3149m *(E of NPI, San Lorenzo)* J Hauf, T Rawson, T Walter, 3 Mar 1987; FA of north summit via N face, *AAJ 30 (1988) 173-174; PMLTM 191*

San Valentin - 4058m *(NPI, San Valentin, Arenales)* D Bertoncelij, B Lantschner, T Pangerc, 18 Dec 1952; FA via SW ridge *AJ 59 (1953) 432-435; PMLTM 183*

Techada Negro - 2173m *(SPI, Fitz Roy)* S Bossini, 28 Feb 1961; *AAJ 12 (1961) 263; PMLTM 228* S Bossini, C Fava, J P Spikermann, 1 Mar 1961; NR via S face, *AAJ 12 (1961) 263; PMLTM 228*

Torre Centrale (Central Tower of Paine) - 2460m *(SPI, Paine)* C Bonington, D Whillans, 16 Jan 1963; FA via N face, *AJ 68 (1963) 179-187; PMLTM 256* M Scott, R Smithers, 21 Jan 1974; NR via E face, *AJ 80 (1975) 5-16; PMLTM 256* A Kearney, R Knight, 2 Jan 1982; NR via S face, *AAJ 24 (1982) 109-217; PMLTM 256* M Giarolli, E Orlandi, E Salvaterra, 31 Oct 1986; NR via SE face, *AAJ 29 (1987) 216; PMLTM 256* F Defrancesco, M Mànica, F Stedile, 2 Nov 1986; NR via NW buttress, *AAJ 29 (1987) 216; PMLTM 256* S Cosgrove, J Smith, 7 Jan 1989; NR via NW arete, *CL #119 (1990) 61* K Albert, B Arnold, W Gullich, 23 Jan 1991; NR via E face, pc

Torre de la Media Luna (spire below El Mocho) *(SPI, Cerro Torre, Cordón Adela)* Kathy Cosley, M Houston, 4 Feb 1988; FA via E face, *AAJ 31 (1989) 178*

Torre Egger - 2900m *(SPI, Cerro Torre, Cordón Adela)* J Bragg, J Donini, J Wilson, 22 Feb 1976; FA via lower E face of Cerro Torre and upper S face of Torre Egger, *AAJ 21 (1977) 49-56; PMLTM 230* B De Donà, G Giongo, 15 Mar 1980; NR via E face, *AAJ 27 (1985) 239; PMLTM 230* J Jeglic, S Karo, F Knez, 7 Dec 986; NR via SE dihedral, *PMLTM 230* M Giarolli, E Orlandi, 5 Nov 1987; NR via E buttress, *AAJ 30 (1988) 53-55*

Torre Nord (North Tower of Paine) - 2260m *(SPI, Paine)* J Bich, L Carrel, C Pelissier, P Pession, 17 Jan 1958; FA via S ridge, *PMLTM 258*

Torre Sud (South Tower of Paine) - 2500m *(SPI, Paine)* J Aiazzi, A Aste, C Casati, N Nusdeo, V Taldo, 9 Feb 1963; FA via N face and N ridge, *PMLTM 254* G Bagatoli, M Cagol, J Espen, F Leoni, 1 Nov 1987; NR via SW ridge *AAJ 31 (1989) 179*

Tridente - 2300m *(SPI, Paine)* V Bray, D Clarke, P Henry, B Page, D Walter, 22 Jan 1961; FA, *AJ 74 (1969) 276; PMLTM 258* I Burgess, S Hillen, D Lister, D Tyson, 27 Oct 1989; NR via NW face, *AAJ 32 (1990) 210*

Trono Blanco (Mellizo Este) - 2430m *(SPI, Paine)* L Horka, P Klimza, G Oyarzún, 21 Feb 1969; FA, *AJ 75 (1970) 236; PMLTM 252*

Volcán Lautaro - 3380m *(SPI, Cordón Lautaro)* L Pera, P Skvarca, 29 Jan196;4, FA from NW, *PMLTM 207* G Chauregui, C Galvez, P Jara, R Labbe, M Munijn, 10 Feb 1986; NR via W face, *AAJ 29 (1987) 206; PMLTM 207*

APPENDIX III

BIBLIOGRAPHY

Abbreviations used include:

AAJ: American Alpine Journal, American Alpine Club, New York
AJ: Alpine Journal, The Alpine Club, London
CAJ: Canadian Alpine Journal, Alpine Club of Canada, Banff
Ascent: Ascent, Sierra Club, San Francisco
Climbing: Climbing Magazine, Aspen, Colorado
JMCSA: Journal of the Mountain Club of South Africa, Cape Town
M: Mountain Magazine, London and Sheffield
MC: Mountain Craft, London
NZAJ: New Zealand Alpine Journal, New Zealand Alpine Club, Dunedin
R&I: Rock & Ice, Boulder, Colorado
Summit: Summit Magazine, Big Bear Lake, California

Journal references are cited as: volume or issue # (year) page(s)

Natural Sciences and Patagonia:

Andrews, M: *The Flight of the Condor,* Boston: Little Brown, 1982
Conner, T M: *Mountain Winds, AJ,* 81 (1976) p81-90
Flint, R F: *Glacial Geology and the Pleistocene Epoch,* NY: John Wiley, 1947
Hough, R: *The Blind Horn's Hate,* NY: Norton, 1971
Mercer, J H: *Glacial History of Southernmost South America,* Quaternary Research, NY, #6 (1976) p125-66
Nordenskjöld, O: *The Geography of the Polar Regions,* NY: American Geographical Society, #8 (1928) p25-27
Saint Exupéry, A De: *Wind, Sand and Stars,* NY: Reynal and Hitchcock, 1939
Shipton, E E: *Land of Tempest,* London: Hodder and Stoughton, 1963
Simpson, G G: *Attending Marvels,* NY: Time, 1934

Ice caps and general references:

Agostini, A M De: *Ande Patagoniche,* Milano: Societa Cartographica Giovanni De Agostini, 1949
Buscaini, G & Metzeltin, S: *Patagonia: Terra Magica Per Alpinisti e Viaggiatori,* Milano: Dall Oglio, 1987
Crew, P (and others): *Climbing in Patagonia, MC,* #81 (Autumn, 1968) p11-39 (includes Fitz Roy and Paine, with articles by Whillans, Maestri, Haston, Bonington, Gregory and Shipton)

Fitz Roy:

Azema, MA: *The Conquest of Fitz Roy,* London: Andre Deutsch, 1957
Capellas, C: *Fitz Roy (Chaltal)* Sabadell: Cuadernos de Alpinismo, 1985, (guidebook; includes Fitz Roy, Poincenot, Rafaél, Mermoz, Guillaumet, St Exupéry)
Carrington, R: *South American Assorted, M,* #58 (Nov/Dec 1977) p18-27
Casarotto, R: *Fitz Roy: Solo on the North Pillar, AAJ,* 22 (1980) p383-386
Chouinard, Y: *Climbing Ice,* San Francisco: Sierra Club, 1978
DeVilliers, B: *Aguja Guillaumet, JMCSA,* (1973)
Dorworth, R: *The Third Ascent of Fitz Roy, Summit,* #8 (Oct 1969) p2-7
(Fitz Roy): *Climbs and Expeditions, AAJ,* 18 (1973) p477
(Fitz Roy & Cerro Torre): *INFO, M,* #101 (Jan/Feb 1985) p10
Fonrouge, J L & Comesaña, C E: *Fitz Roy by the Supercouloir, AAJ,* 15 (1966) p75-80
Fuggle, R: *The Fight Against Fitz Roy, JMCSA,,* (1973)
Gallego, M A: *Fitz Roy, M,* #103 (May/Jun 1985) p20-23
Harrington, S: *Saint Exupéry,* Climbing, #110 (Oct 1988) p72-76

Holdener, T: *Fitz Roy: Climb Without a Summit, M,* #38 (Sep 1974) p32-33
Jones, C: *The Southwest Buttress of Fitz Roy, M,* #3 (1969) p8-15
Karl, R: *A Close Call on Fitz Roy, Climbing,* #74 (Sep/Oct 1982) p22-27
Kearney, A: *Fitz Roy and Cerro Torre, Climbing,* #90 (Jun 1985) p36-43
——: *Fitz Roy and Cerro Torre, AAJ,* 28 (1986) p101-109
Motti, G P: *Singular Success: the Solo Climbs of Renato Casarotto, M,* #95
    (Jan/Feb 1984) p26-33
Nicol, D: *Fitz Roy's South Buttress, M,* #28 (Jul 1973) p19-21
Orolin, M: *Fitz Roy: West Face, M,* #95 (Jan/Feb 1984) p20-25
Rouse, A: *A Patagonian Holiday, Climbing,* #47 (Mar/Apr 1978) p5-11
Terray, L: *Conquistadors of the Useless,* London: Gollancz, 1963
Tompkins, D R: *Fitz Roy 1968, AAJ,* 16 (1969) p263-269
Whillans, D: *Aiguille Poincenot, AJ,* 67 (1962) p236-242
——: *Don Whillans Mountain Interview, M,* #20 (Mar 1972) p24-28
——: *Don Whillans, Portrait of a Mountaineer,* London: Heinemann, 1971

Cerro Torre:
Bonatti, W: *On the Heights,* London: Hart-Davis, 1964 & Diadem, 1979
Bragg, J: *Cerro Torre Revisited, R&I,* #3 p7-11
——: *Torre Egger, AAJ,* 21 (1977) p49-56
Brewer, S: *Cerro Torre: Alpine Style, Climbing,* #58 (Jan/Feb 1980) p24-28
Bridwell, J: *Cerro Torre: Alpine Style, AAJ,* 22 (1980) p375-382
——: *Riders On The Storm, R&I,* #32 (Jul/Aug 1989) p18-27
Burke, P: *Cerro Torre: East Face, M,* #79 (May/Jun 1981) p40-42
Campbell-Kelly, B (& Wyvill, B): *Patagonia Handbook: Cerro Stanhardt, 1974/5
    Report of the 1974 Patagonian Mountaineering Expedition, 1975*
(Cerro Stanhardt): Climbs and Expeditions, AAJ, 20 (1976) p503-504
Cerro Torre: A Mountain Desecrated, M, #23 (Sep 1972) p20-26
(Cerro Torre): *Climbs and Expeditions, AAJ,* 33 (1959) p317-318
(Cerro Torre, East Face): *Climbs and Expeditions, AAJ,* 24 (1982) p193-194
Crew, P: *The British Cerro Torre Expedition, AJ,* 73 (1969) p186-198
Denz, B: *Headwall, NZAJ,* 34 (1981)
Dickinson, L: *Filming the Impossible,* London: Jonathan Cape, 1982
Donini, J: *The Torre Egger Climb, M,* #51 (Sep/Oct 1976) p19-25
——: *To Torre Egger's Icy Summit, National Geographic,* Washington, 1977
Ferrari, C: *Cerro Torre Climbed, M,* #38 (Sep 1974) p26-29
Haston, D: *In High Places, New York: Macmillan, 1973*
Heppenstall, A: *Further thoughts on the Cerro Torre problem, M,* #42 (Mar/Apr
    1975) p38-43
Maestri, C: *Cerro Torre: Maestri Speaks Again, M,* #18 (Nov 1971)
——: *Mountain Interview, M,* #23 (Sep 1972) p30-37
——: *The Cerro Torre Enigma: Maestri Speaks, M,* #9 (May 1970) p32
——: *The Conquest of Cerro Torre, MC,* #81 (Autumn 1968) p22-25
——: *The Southeast Ridge of Cerro Torre, M,* #16 (Jul 1971) p23-24
Mauri, C: *Cerro Torre: The West Face, M,* #11 (Sep 1970) p17-23
Pedrini, M: *Patagonia "A La Carte", M,* #110 (Jul/Aug 1986) p20-23
Rouse, A: *Cerro Stanhardt, Aguja Poincenot, Cuatro Dedos, Gran Gendarme de
    Pollone and Other Peaks in the Fitz Roy Area, AAJ,* 21 (1978) p581-583
Thomson, D: *Torre Egger Retrospect, NZAJ,* 30 (1977) p62-65
Tompkins, D: article in Ascent, Sierra Club, San Francisco, 1971

Paine:
Aste, A: *Premire ascension de la Tour sud du Paine, Les Alpes,* Swiss Alpine
    Club, 40 (1964) p226-234
Bonington, C: *The Central Tower of Paine, AJ,* 68 (1963) p179-187
——: *The Next Horizon,* London: Gollancz, 1973
Cheesemond, D: *The Mummer-Cordillera del Paine, Chile, AJ,* 84 (1979)
    p117-118

Clough, I:*The First Ascent of the Fortress and Future Prospects in the Cordillera del Paine, AJ,* 73 (1968) p143-157
Clough, I & Whillans, D:*Central Tower of Paine, AAJ,* 38 (1964) p86-90
(Cuerno Principal):*Climbs and Expeditions, AAJ,* 43 (1969) p446
Davies, H:*The East.Face Of Paine Grande, Patagonia, JMCSA,* (1986)
Fatti, P:*Cordillera del Paine, JMCSA,(1972)*

Fortress, East Buttress:
INFO, M, #66 (Mar/Apr 1979) p11
Kearney, A:*Central Tower of Paine, AAJ,* 24 (1982) p109-117
——:*Forty Hours on the Central Tower of Paine, Climbing,* #72 (May/Jun 1982) p10-15
Knight, R:*Dreams and Doubts: Six Weeks in the Paine Cordillera, Ascent,* (1984) p116-129
McGarr, A:*East Face of the Central Tower of Paine, AAJ,* 20 (1975) p101-107
Monzino, G:*Italia in Patagonia,* Milan: Martello, 1958, (Paine Grande Principal; North Tower of Paine)
Nicol, D:*Suddenly Last Summer, M,* #16 (Jul 1971) p15-21
(Paine Chico):*Various Notes, AAJ,* 3 (1938) p227
(Paine Grande):*INFO, M,* #105 (Sep/Oct 1985) p15
(Paine Group):*Climbs and Expeditions, AAJ,* 10 (1956) p132-134
(Paine Towers):*Climbs and Expeditions, AAJ,* 13 (1963) p515-516
Scott, M:*At the Eleventh Hour, AJ,* 80 (1975) p5-16
——:*Climbing the Sword, JMCSA,* (1972)
——:*The Eleventh Hour, Climbing,* (Winter, 1974-75) p2-7, p38-44

For additional foreign language items, see the extensive bibliography in Jill Neate's *Mountaineering in the Andes: a Source Book for Climbers,* London: Expedition Advisory Centre, 1987, p246-257

PHOTOGRAPHY

This book contains the finest climbs in Patagonia; those that have contributed to the mystique of the region. But words alone are woefully inadequate to convey my fondness for these mountains. The photographs obtained with my *Nikon* FM and a single 24mm or 20mm wide angle lens are, for the most part, a record of events taking place during a major technical ascent. On the mountain I kept my equipment minimal, to remain unobtrusive. Climbing partners often don't appreciate being asked to stop what they're doing in the midst of a demanding pitch. One can usually be discreet, but co-operation from the model is sometimes essential to obtaining interesting photographs.

In the majority of climbing films, a lot of staging takes place to produce stunning footage. The fact that a fixed rope is anchored above for the cameraman detracts from the authenticity and motives for the ascent but may add to the drama. Are the participants there to climb the mountain or to make a film? Objectives often get confused. When planning their adventure, climbers must decide what has priority and agree to work towards that goal. Expedition style climbing with fixed ropes lends itself better to film making or shooting still photographs, as the cameramen can move independently of the lead climber. Alpine style ascents use practically no fixed rope and the photographer is limited to a few camera angles. In 1968, however, the American group on Fitz Roy made a fine film of their ascent without using the expeditionary techniques mentioned above.

In my photographs, things happened just as you see them. I didn't climb back up any fixed ropes on Cerro Torre in a storm to shoot more film of ropes blowing all over the place; I got the hell off the mountain! I find it challenging to try to capture the essence of a climb on film without expedition support or pre-placed fixed ropes.

Authentic images can be very powerful. There are no multiple exposures in these photographs of Patagonia, just lots of effort selecting the best light and anticipating potential photographic opportunities. All of the frames were shot with *Kodachrome 64* and *Fujichrome Velvia* (ASA 50) at the recommended ASA. No special filters were used except for normal ultraviolet filters to protect the lenses and compensate slightly for the excessive blue inherent in mountain photographs. When hiking the countryside or photographing from the forest, lenses used included the 16mm, 20mm, 24mm, 55mm macro, 43-86 zoom, 105mm, 135mm, 300mm ED, and 600mm ED with *Nikon FM, F2 and F3* camera bodies.

I hope the climbing history, my personal experiences, and my photographs may help others appreciate Patagonia as I do.

GLOSSARY

Ablation: the melting away of a glacier

Abseil (Ger): see *Rappel*

Aguja (Sp): needle; a sharply pointed peak

Aid: slang for direct aid or artificial climbing

Alpine hammer: short hammer with a pick for driving pitons or climbing ice

Alpine-style: climbing peaks in a single push without established camps, support from other climbing members or fixed ropes

Anchor: means of fastening or threading a climbing rope to ice or rock using either an ice screw, bolt, piton, nut or camming device

Angle: slang for angle piton

Angle piton: piton manufactured in sizes from 125mm to 375mm in width for driving into cracks

Arête (Fr): a sharp ridge on a mountain Ascender: a mechanical device for gripping and climbing a rope

Belay: means whereby a stationary climber pays out rope to another and applies friction to the rope should the moving climber fall

Bergschrund (Ger): a large crevasse formed by tension where flowing ice of a glacier fractures away from a nearly stagnant ice slope or headwall above

Big wall: a vertical or nearly vertical face that requires two days or more to ascend; and where hauling techniques are usually employed to move equipment up

Bivouac: temporary encampment during a climb; varies from several hours to overnight

Bivy: slang for bivouac

Bolt: an anchor placed into a drilled hole to protect or climb a portion of a route that cannot be done by pitons

Bolt ladder: a series of bolts 1 to 2 meters apart on a rock wall

Bong: a large piton manufactured in sizes from 5cm to 10cm in width

Brazo (Sp): arm, as of a lake

Buttress: a major formation on a peak that is broader than an arête

Carabiner (Ger): metal snaplink for clipping a rope to anchors

Ceiling: see *Overhang*

Cerro (Sp): mountain; usually denotes a peak below the permanent snow line

Chimney: a deep slot 30cm to 2 meters in width

Chute: a depression steeper than a gully

Clean: removal of the anchors from a pitch by a second climber

Clog: an aluminum or brass nut for wedging into cracks

Col: a steep high pass, smaller than a saddle

Continental Ice: refers to a large permanent ice sheet with glaciers flowing off the perimeters

Copperhead: a small nut made of copper that is knocked into cracks for aid climbing

Corner: see *Dihedral*

Cornice: an overhanging ledge of snow that forms at the tops of gullies, and on the leeward side of ridges or summits

Couloir (Fr): a deep chute that is likely to have snow or ice in it Crack: an opening or fissure in rock

Crampons: twelve-spiked metal frames attached to boots for climbing ice

Crevasse: a deep crack or fissure in the ice of a glacier

Cumbre (Sp): summit

Dièdre (Fr): see *Dihedral*

Dihedral: an inside corner or open book; a depression, generally open 90 degrees or more on its facings, as a junction of two rock planes an angular slab lying against a flat wall may form a left-facing or right-facing open book

Direct aid: involves the use of any artificial means of ascent, not relying completely on hands and feet

Estancia (Sp): Argentine or Chilean ranch

Étrier (Fr): see *Stirrup*

Expedition-style: means of ascending a mountain that relies on a gradual buildup and stocking of camps on the mountainside; usually requires a group of climbers and much fixed rope to insure safe travel between camps

Face: a steep mountainside, generally over 30 degrees if mixed snow, ice, and rock; and over 45 degrees if rock

Face climbing: type of climbing whereby one uses fingertips and boot edges, to cling to, and stand on, knobs and crystals of rock; a type of Free Climbing

Fault: a fracture in the earth's crust resulting in the relative displacement of the rocks on either side of it

Fin: a rock or ice feature more slender than a gendarme

Finger lock: a type of jam where the tips of the fingers are wedged in a crack

Fix: to anchor rope to a mountainside for later use

Flake: a thin and sometimes fragile wafer of rock on a face or wall; may be very large

Free climbing: means that no direct support from piton, stirrup, loop, rope, or carabiner is used; any such pieces of equipment may be used for safety only; free climbing may be roped or unroped

Friend: a spring-loaded camming device used as an anchor in cracks of varying widths

Front point: to ascend ice using only the forward points on one's crampons and the picks of ice tools

Fumarole: a vent in snow and ice, caused by the heat from magma close to the surface, in a volcano; often accompanied by steam and sulphurous gases

Gale: a strong wind from 62 to 79 kilometers per hour

Gaucho (Sp): Argentine cowboy or horseman

Gendarme (Fr): a sharp pinnacle of rock on a mountain ridge that is often difficult to climb around or over

Glacier: a body of ice that has sufficient mass and downward slope to move

Granite: a coarse-grained igneous rock consisting mainly of quartz and feldspar

Gully: a depression grooving a mountainside

Hardware: a collection of anchors used in ascending an ice or rock face

Haul bag: either a rucksack or duffelbag used to haul bivouac equipment and food up a face

Haul line: a rope between 6 and 9 millimeters in diameter, used for rappelling or pulling up equipment

Headwall: where the slope or face of a mountain, cirque or glacier steepens dramatically in angle; also, the final sheer wall below the summit

Hemp: a natural fiber used in manufacturing early climbing ropes; when new hemp ropes have about 700 kilos breaking strength

Hexentric: an offset California-made, hex shaped aluminum wedge for placing in cracks as an anchor

Hex nut: hexagonal shaped aluminum wedge

Ice axe: tool with a shaft between 50 and 80 centimeters in length, with a sharp pick for climbing ice and a small axe blade for chopping

Ice cap: see *Continental Ice*

Ice fall: a steep reach of glacier with a chaotic crevassed surface and rapid flow rate

Ice hammer: see *Alpine Hammer*

Ice mushroom: a bulbous cap of ice and snow formed by rime deposition, that cloaks many Patagonian summits

Ice screw: a tubular, threaded, metal anchor that is twisted into ice

Jam: to wedge hands and feet into a crack when free climbing

Jumar: a Swiss made mechanical ascender

Knifeblade: a thin short piton

Lago (Sp): lake

Lead: see *Pitch*

Ledge or ramp: a narrow shelf on a mountainside that generally runs some distance; a ramp is an ascending ledge

Lieback: free climbing technique used on flakes and in dihedrals, whereby one pushes against a wall with the feet and pulls back on an edge with the hands

Line: slang for rope

Lowe camming nut: a spring-loaded camming device for cracks; a precursor to *Friends*

Mixed: used to describe a face that must be climbed using snow, ice and rock techniques

Névé (Fr): consolidated granular snow in the state of transition to glacier ice; glacier snowfield; also refers to hard or frozen snow

North wall hammer: an ice tool between 45 and 55 centimeters in length with a curved pick for climbing ice and a hammer head for pounding ice screws or pitons

Notch: generally a narrow col or sharp break in a ridge

Nut: wedge-shaped aluminum chockstone for slotting into cracks as an anchor

Nylon: ropes made from nylon filaments, comprising three twisted strands and having a breaking strength of between 900 and 1400 kilos

Offwidth: a large crack between 12.5cm and 30cm in width

Overhang: a section of wall above the angle of 90 degrees; termed ceiling or roof when nearly 180 degrees

Pampas: the dry scrub and grasslands in the rainshadow of the mountains of southern Argentina

Pedestal: a pillar of rock that leans against or is part of a rock wall

Pendulum: a swinging traverse made from a fixed point

Perlon: synthetic filaments woven into a bundle of core fibers and covered with a sheath; ropes of Perlon are stronger than nylon, stretch less in normal use and are easier to handle

Pile: lightweight synthetic material used in jackets and pants that retains its insulating properties when wet

Pillar: a mountain formation that is usually rounded and sharply defined

Pin: slang for piton

Piolet (Fr): see *Ice Axe*

Pitch: section of the climb between belays; length can vary from a short distance to the full length of a climbing rope; most pitches vary from 25 to 50 meters. Sometimes called a Lead

Piton: metal spike driven into a crack for an anchor (see *Angle, Bong, Knifeblade and Rurp)*

Protection: any type of anchor placed on lead that minimizes a fall

Prusik: to ascend a rope using prusik knots

Prusik knot: a slip knot which, when attached to a rope, will not move when loaded

Punta (Sp): point, such as a sharp mountain summit

Ramp: see *Ledge*

Rappel (Fr): to descend (slide down) using a rope and friction device

Rib: an edge on a rock face; a shallow buttress

Rio (Sp): river

Rivet: a short aluminum nail, pounded into a shallow hole drilled in blank rock; the rivet is then used as an anchor for aid climbing

Rock hammer: a one-kilo hammer used for driving pitons or placing bolts

Rock shoe: supple rubber-soled shoes for climbing rock; in Patagonia, rock shoes are often worn inside plastic outer boots, for rapid exchange when conditions alter

Rope length: see *Pitch*

Route: the line or path climbers follow up a mountainside

Rucksack: sack with shoulder straps for carrying equipment

Rurp: a tiny piton used for direct aid

Saddle: a more rounded ridge depression than a col; can be wide and almost flat

Sérac (Fr): a block tower or pinnacle of ice or hard snow formed by the intersection of crevasses, or found standing in ice falls

Siege: see *Expedition-style*

Sling: a loop of nylon webbing

Snout: the very tip of an advancing or retreating glacier Solo: to climb a mountain alone

Spindrift: powdery snow driven by wind or washed down by avalanches

Spur: subsidary ridge branching from a larger ridge

Stance: small ledge on which a climber belays

Stem: to use counterpressure with the hands and feet in a corner

Stirrup: a three-runged nylon or aluminum ladder used for aid climbing

Stopper: a California-made aluminum nut for wedging into cracks

Storm: a wind ranging from 100 to 115 kilometers per hour

Super box: a type of box tent that can be suspended from a big wall

Talus: rock rubble that forms slopes at the base of mountain faces

Tension: leaning against a taut rope to rest while free climbing or using tension as a tool in aid climbing

Torre (Sp): tower

Valley glacier: a glacier that occupies a valley and is scouring away rock on both sides and beneath the ice

Verglas (Fr): water ice; a veneer of ice that covers rock faces after a storm

Vortex: a whirling mass or motion of gas

Webbing: flat nylon tape 125mm to 250mm in width used in climbing

Wooden wedges: driven into large cracks and used for anchors before the advent of aluminum bongs and camming devices